FROM EARTH
TO PLATE

FROM EARTH TO PLATE

Cooking with root vegetables

Denise McGuigan

Contents

Introduction 7

Soups 9

Entrées 57

Mains 83

Sides 123

Index 174

Introduction

Root vegetables are a staple food in the western world and a major component of our diets. Little wonder really. These inexpensive vegetables are very easy to grow and are farmed in vast quantities. This is food that feeds everybody. Carrots, potatoes, onions, parsnips, garlic and beetroot are just a few of the everyday vegetables known as roots and they deserve to be given fresh consideration.

Because these vegetables spend their entire growing life underground, they are densely packed with nutrition, all absorbed from the soil in which they grow. We all know that eating a varied diet made up predominantly of vegetables is known to boost health, and what better way to begin than incorporating plenty of these roots into your everyday menu planning? Eaten fresh from the garden, these vegetables taste sweet and are brimming with vitality. Individually these vegetables contain beneficial carbohydrates that release their energy slowly into the bloodstream helping to keep you feeling full for longer. The additional benefit for the cook though, is that they have a longer storage value and as long as they are kept in a cool, dark place, they will keep well and retain their nutritional value.

Root vegetables can be grated, diced and sliced. Cooked fresh from the garden, they don't even need peeling, just a vigorous scrub under running water will do, since much of the nutrition lies just beneath the surface of the skin. Try them steamed and served with butter, boiled and mashed, roasted whole, or baked and liquidised into soup, curried with spices, or even chipped. Eat fresh carrots and onions raw, or bring out their flavour with gentle cooking.

If you're short of ideas, want to ring the changes, or just try different vegetables, this cookbook is brimming with ideas and tried-and-tested recipes to help get your started. Happy cooking.

Soups

Rich vegetable stock

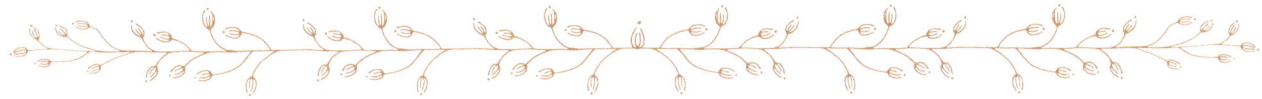

2 tablespoons olive oil
1 turnip or swede, peeled and chopped
5 garlic cloves
3 celery stalks, scrubbed
3 large carrots, peeled
10 mushrooms, wiped
3 large onions, peeled
4 tomatoes
2 leeks, washed and sliced
2 parsnips, peeled
8 Brussels sprouts, peeled
10 sprigs parsley
1 teaspoon peppercorns
4 bay leaves
salt, to taste

makes 2 litres/3½ pints/8 cups

Heat the olive oil in a large stockpot and sauté all the vegetables, for 20 minutes, until they develop a golden tone on their surface.s

Add the parsley, peppercorns, bay leaves and 4 litres/7 pints of water to cover and bring to the boil. Simmer for 3 hours, skimming the surface to remove any scum that accumulates.

Add salt to taste, and continue to simmer until reduced in volume by half. Allow to cool then remove and discard the vegetables. Use within three days or freeze in batches for up to 12 months.

NOTE: In addition to the vegetables listed, you can add any other vegetables that are past their prime – greens, root vegetables, corn and bell peppers all work well.

Soups

Brown onion and egg yolk soup

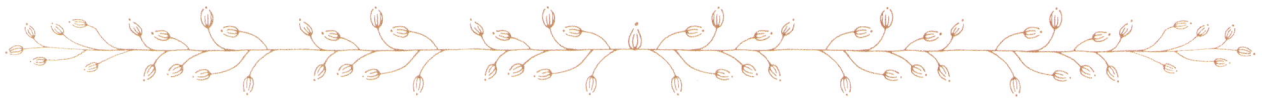

50 g (1¾ oz) butter
600 g (1¼ lb) onions, peeled and sliced
2 litres (3½ pints/8 cups) beef stock
2 tablespoons (¼ cup) parsley, chopped
1 teaspoon salt
generous pinch of cayenne pepper
nutmeg, to taste
3 egg yolks
60 ml (2 fl oz/¼ cup) port

serves 6

Melt the butter in a deep heavy pan and when the butter is foaming add the onions. Fry the onions until dark brown without burning, stirring constantly.

Add the stock and bring to the boil. Boil for 45 minutes and then add the parsley, salt, cayenne pepper and nutmeg. Return to the boil and cook for another 10 minutes.

To serve, pour the soup into a tureen and keep hot.

Mix the egg yolks with the port in a sauceboat. Pour the egg yolk mixture into the soup while stirring and serve immediately with crusty bread.

Easy French onion soup

55 g/2 oz butter
750 g/1 lb 11 oz onions, peeled and thinly sliced
1 garlic clove, peeled and crushed
2 teaspoons plain (all-purpose) flour
1.25 litres/2¼ pints/5 cups beef stock
salt and freshly ground black pepper
4 slices French bread, about 25 mm/1 in thick
55 g/2 oz Gruyère cheese, grated

serves 4

Heat the butter in a large heavy pan set over low heat until it melts and begins to foam. Add the onions and garlic, cover the pan, then fry, for 30–35 minutes, until the onions are golden brown. Stir often to stop the onions from sticking to the base of the pan.

Add the flour and cook, stirring constantly, for 2–3 minutes. Pour in the stock little by little, stirring all the time, and bring to the boil. Reduce the heat and simmer, covered, for 30 minutes. Season to taste with salt and black pepper.

Preheat the grill (broiler) to high. Toast the French bread on one side under the grill, then top the uncooked side with the grated cheese. Grill (broil) until the cheese has melted and browned. Pour the soup into individual bowls and place a slice of the cheese-topped toasted bread on top of each serving.

NOTE: The secret with this soup is to cook the onions long enough to give them a brown colour, without burning the butter. The browner the onions, the sweeter and richer the soup will be. Adding 2 teaspoons of sugar to the onions after 10 minutes makes them brown faster.

Leek, potato and bacon soup

2.5 kg (5½ lb) potatoes, peeled and cut into chunks
2 leeks, sliced into 3 cm (1¼ in) rings
500 g (1 lb 2 oz) bacon, chopped
salt and freshly ground black pepper, to taste
300 ml (½ pint) sour cream
2 or 3 shallots, chopped
¼ cup (2 tablespoons) coriander (cilantro), chopped

serves 4-6

Place the potatoes in a large pan with enough water to cover. Bring the water to the boil and cook the potatoes for about 10 minutes, or until soft. Use a slotted spoon to transfer the potatoes to a large bowl. Retain the potato water.

Mash the potatoes with some saved water (the mixture should have the consistency of thick soup).

Return the mashed potatoes to the pan with the leek and bacon and simmer until the leek is soft and the bacon is cooked. Season with salt and pepper.

In a bowl, mix the sour cream and shallots. Serve hot, garnished with coriander and sour cream and shallots.

Provençal-style soup with onion pesto

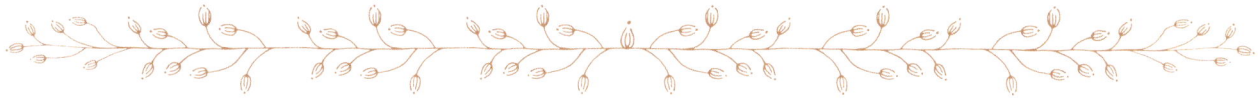

2 tablespoons extra virgin olive oil
1 onion, chopped
1 medium potato, peeled and chopped
1 carrot, chopped
1 yellow capsicum (bell pepper), deseeded and chopped
500 ml (17 fl oz/2 cups) vegetable stock
2 stalks celery, chopped
2 courgettes (zucchini), chopped
400 g (14 oz) can tomatoes
1 tablespoon tomato purée
salt and ground black pepper

FOR THE ONION PESTO
6 scallions (spring onions), roughly chopped
50 g (1¾oz) Parmesan, grated
4 tablespoons extra virgin olive oil

Heat the oil in a large heavy pan, then add the onion, potato, carrot and yellow capsicum. Cook, uncovered, for 5 minutes, over a medium heat, stirring occasionally, until the vegetables start to brown.

Add the stock, celery and courgettes and bring to the boil. Cover and simmer for 10 minutes, or until the vegetables are tender. Stir in the tomatoes, tomato purée and season generously. Simmer uncovered for 10 minutes.

Meanwhile, make the pesto. Place the scallions, Parmesan and oil in a food processor and process together to a fairly smooth paste. Ladle the soup into bowls and top with a spoonful of the pesto.

serves 4-6

Borscht

3 tablespoons sunflower oil or butter
2 large onions, finely diced
2 medium carrots, peeled and diced
1 parsnip, peeled and diced
500 g (1 lb 2 oz) chuck steak cut into 2 cm (¾ in) cubes
2 litres/3½ pints beef stock
2 bay leaves
½ teaspoon dried thyme
salt and pepper, to taste
1 small cabbage, shredded
3 large ripe tomatoes, skinned and diced
3 large raw beetroots, peeled and coarsely grated
Sour cream, for serving
1 tablespoon finely chopped dill

Heat half of the oil in a medium pan, add the diced onions, carrots and parsnip and fry gently, while stirring for 5 minutes, until lightly coloured and aromatic.

Heat a large heavy pan over medium-high heat. Add the remaining oil and meat cubes. Stir to brown the meat on all sides. Add the beef stock, bay leaves, thyme and seasoning, turn the heat down to a simmer and cook, covered, for 30 minutes. Add the shredded cabbage and tomatoes and simmer for another 30 minutes.

Add the beetroot and continue to simmer for 20 minutes. Taste and adjust the seasoning.

Serve in soup bowls with a generous spoon of sour cream and scattering of chopped dill.

serves 6–10

Soups

Creamed borscht

4 medium beetroots
1 litre/1¾ pints/4 cups chicken stock
1 onion, peeled and studded with 4 cloves
1 bouquet garni
1 tablespoon sugar
1 tablespoon lemon juice
salt
60 ml/2 fl oz/¼ cup sour cream

serves 8

Peel and slice 3 of the beetroots. Put in a pan with the stock, onion and bouquet garni and cook over medium heat until quite tender.

Meanwhile, cook the remaining beetroot, without peeling, in boiling water until tender. Allow to cool, peel and grate or cut into julienne strips. Set aside.

Discard the herbs and onion from the sliced beetroot, Purée the cooked beetroot with the stock. Add the sugar, lemon juice, salt and the grated beetroot. Chill thoroughly. Garnish with a spoonful of sour cream to serve.

Soups

Watercress and potato soup

1 kg (2¼ lb) potatoes, peeled and roughly chopped
1 litre (1¾ pints/4 cups) milk
625 ml (generous 1 pint/ 1¼ cups) vegetable stock
1 medium bunch watercress, coarsely chopped
salt and freshly ground black pepper
dill or fennel leaves, chopped, to garnish
croutons and sour cream, to serve

serves 4

Simmer the potatoes in the milk and stock. Add the watercress when the potatoes are nearly cooked, then cook for another 10 minutes.

Purée the ingredients in a the bowl of a blender or food processor. Season with salt and pepper, and chill completely. Serve with the chopped fennel or dill leaves. Serve with croutons and sour cream, if you like.

Root vegetables and pea soup

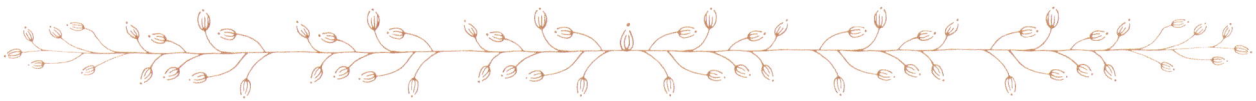

250 g (9 oz) split peas
500 g (1 lb 2 oz) bacon bones
2 carrots, roughly chopped
2 turnips, roughly chopped
2 onions, roughly chopped
4 stalks celery, chopped
salt and freshly ground black pepper
1 tablespoon plain (all-purpose) flour, mixed with 1 tablespoon water
croutons, to serve

serves 8

Wash the peas and soak them in a bowl of water overnight. Drain and rinse. Put the peas and bones in a large pan. Fill the pan two-thirds full with water and bring to the boil. Add the prepared vegetables and simmer for 1½ hours.

Remove the bones using a slotted spoon. Purée the mixture, and season with salt and pepper. Thicken with the flour paste, if needed then, stirring continuously, cook for 3 minutes. Garnish with croutons and serve immediately.

Curried lentil soup

2 tablespoons extra-virgin olive oil
1 onion, chopped
2 teaspoons curry powder
½ teaspoon turmeric
½ teaspoon ground cumin
2 teaspoons tomato paste
1 litre/1¾ pints/4 cups vegetable stock
90 g/3 oz red or green lentils
1 small head broccoli, broken into florets
1 carrot, chopped
1 parsnip, chopped
1 stalk celery, chopped
salt and freshly ground black pepper
1 tablespoon fresh parsley, chopped

Heat the oil in a large pan, add the onion, curry powder, turmeric and cumin and cook, stirring occasionally, for 4–5 minutes, or until the onion is soft. Stir in the tomato paste and stock and bring to the boil. Reduce the heat, add the lentils, cover and simmer for 30 minutes.

Add the broccoli, carrot, parsnip and celery and cook, covered, for 30 minutes more, or until the vegetables are tender.

Season to taste with black pepper and salt. Just prior to serving stir in parsley.

serves 4

Potato and bean soup

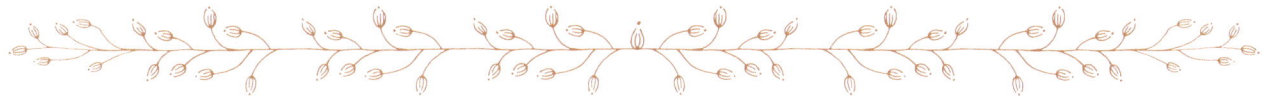

200 g/7 oz dried haricot beans, soaked overnight
1 tablespoon oil
2 onions, chopped
2 cloves garlic, crushed
2 carrots, chopped
2 stalks celery, sliced
2 potatoes, chopped
400 g/14 oz can chopped tomatoes, mashed
¼ cup/2 tablespoons fresh parsley, chopped
freshly ground black pepper

Drain the beans and put them in a large pan with enough water to cover and bring to the boil. Boil for 10 minutes, reduce the heat and simmer for 1 hour, or until the beans are soft. Drain and reserve 500 ml/17 fl oz/2 cups of cooking water. Pour the reserved cooking water and half the beans into the bowl of a food processor or blender and process until smooth.

Heat the oil in a large pan, add the onions and garlic and cook, stirring, for 4–5 minutes, or until the onions are soft. Add the carrots, celery, potatoes, tomatoes, 1.5 litres/2¼ pints/ 6 cups of water, the whole beans and bean purée and bring to the boil. Reduce the heat and simmer for 20 minutes, or until the vegetables are tender. Stir in the parsley and season to taste with black pepper.

serves 4

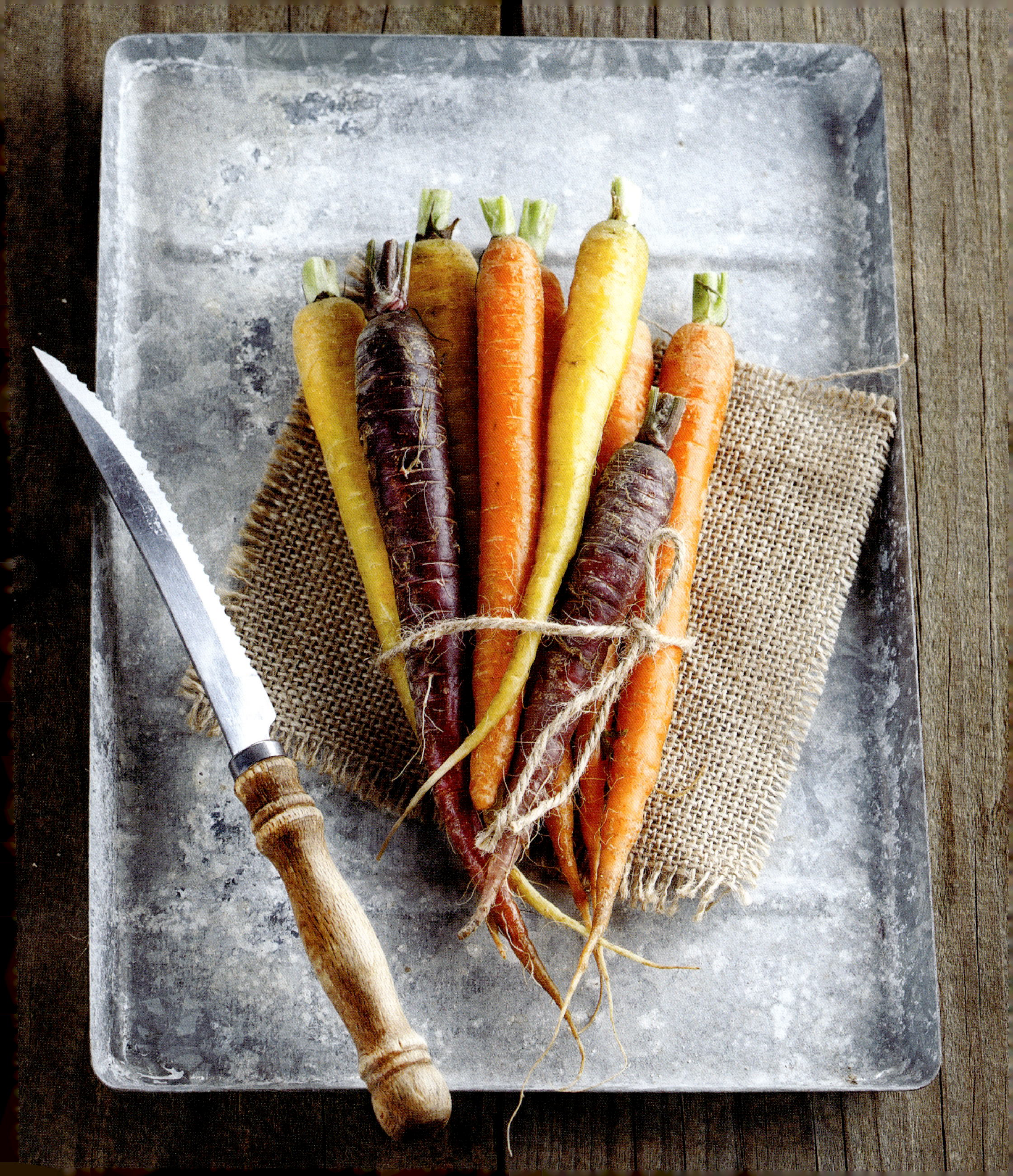

Cumin-spiced carrot soup

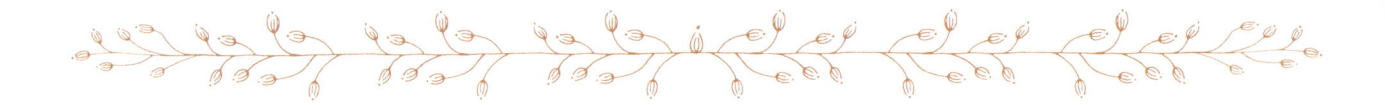

1 tablespoon olive oil
1 large onion, chopped
1 garlic clove, crushed
3 celery sticks, chopped
1 tablespoon ground cumin
700 g/1½ lbs carrots, thinly sliced
900 ml/1½ pints vegetable stock
black pepper
fresh coriander (cilantro), to garnish

Serves 4

Heat the oil in a large saucepan, add the onion, garlic and celery and fry gently for 5 minutes, or until softened, stirring occasionally. Add the cumin and fry, stirring, for 1 minute to release its flavour.

Add the carrots, stock and black pepper to the onion mixture and stir to combine. Bring to the boil and simmer, covered but stirring occasionally, for 30–35 minutes, until the vegetables are tender.

Remove the pan from the heat and cool for a few minutes. Purée the soup until smooth in the bowl of a food processor, liquidiser, or with a hand blender. Return to a clean pan and reheat gently. Serve garnished with fresh coriander.

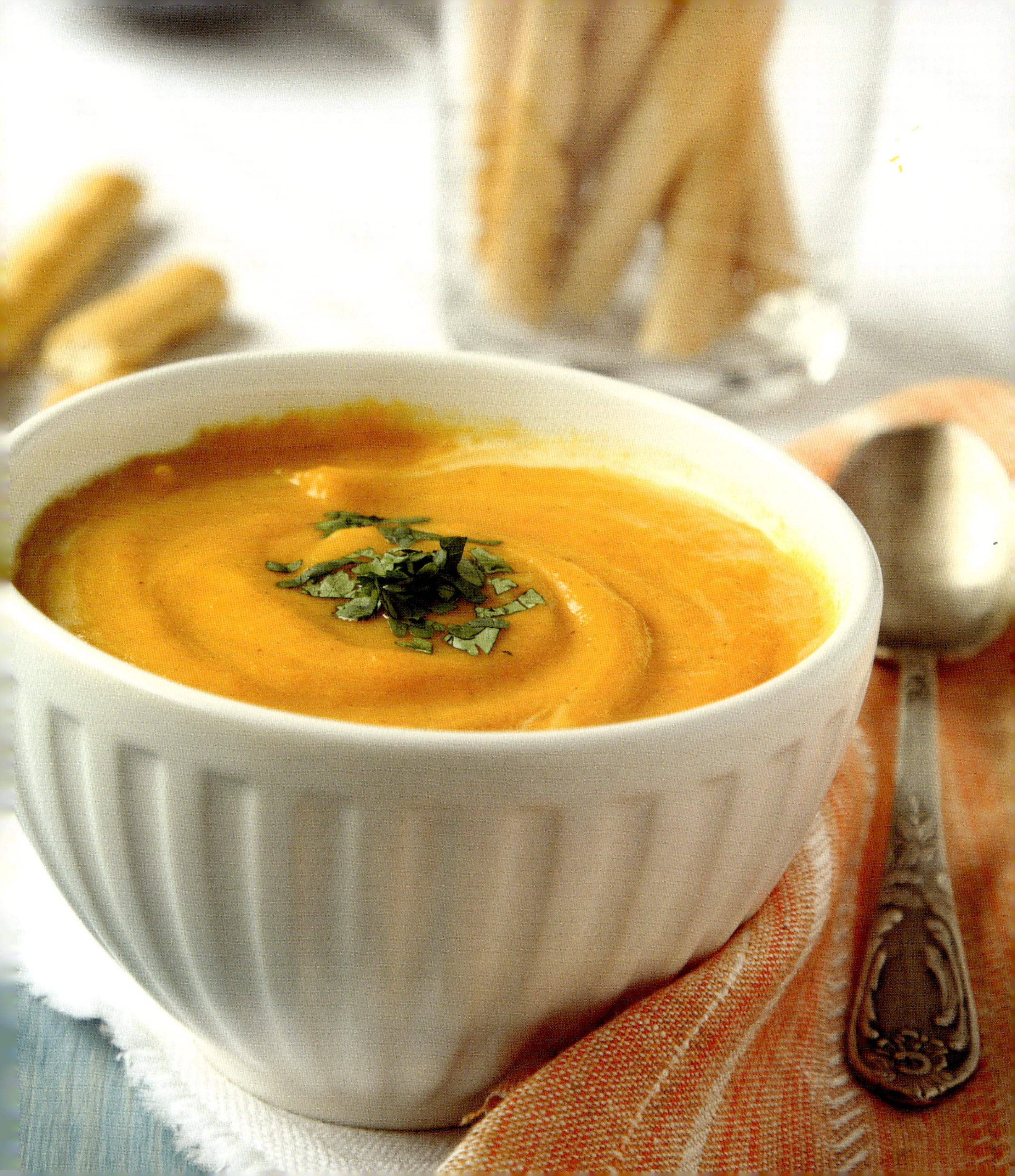

Carrot and lentil soup

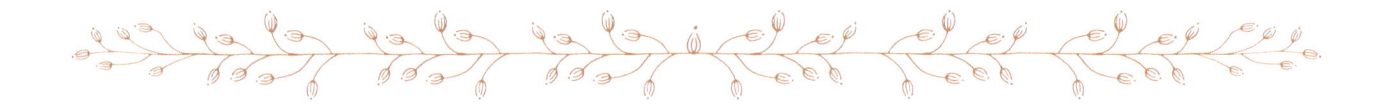

25 g/¾ oz butter
1 tablespoon sunflower oil
450 g/1 lb carrots, sliced
1 onion, chopped
2 sticks celery, chopped
100 g/3½ oz split red lentils, rinsed
850 ml/29 fl oz vegetable stock
sea salt and freshly ground black pepper
natural (plain) yogurt, to garnish
fresh parsley, chopped, to garnish

serves 4

Melt the butter with the oil in a large pan and fry the carrots, onion and celery for 6–8 minutes ,or until lightly golden. Add the lentils and 750 ml/25 fl oz of the vegetable stock and bring to the boil. Cover and simmer for about 20 minutes, until the carrots are tender.

Allow the soup to cool for about 15 minutes, then purée until smooth in the bowl of a liquidiser or food processor. Return to a clean pan with the remaining stock, add seasoning to taste and reheat gently. Add a dollop of yogurt and a scattering of chopped fresh parsley, to garnish.

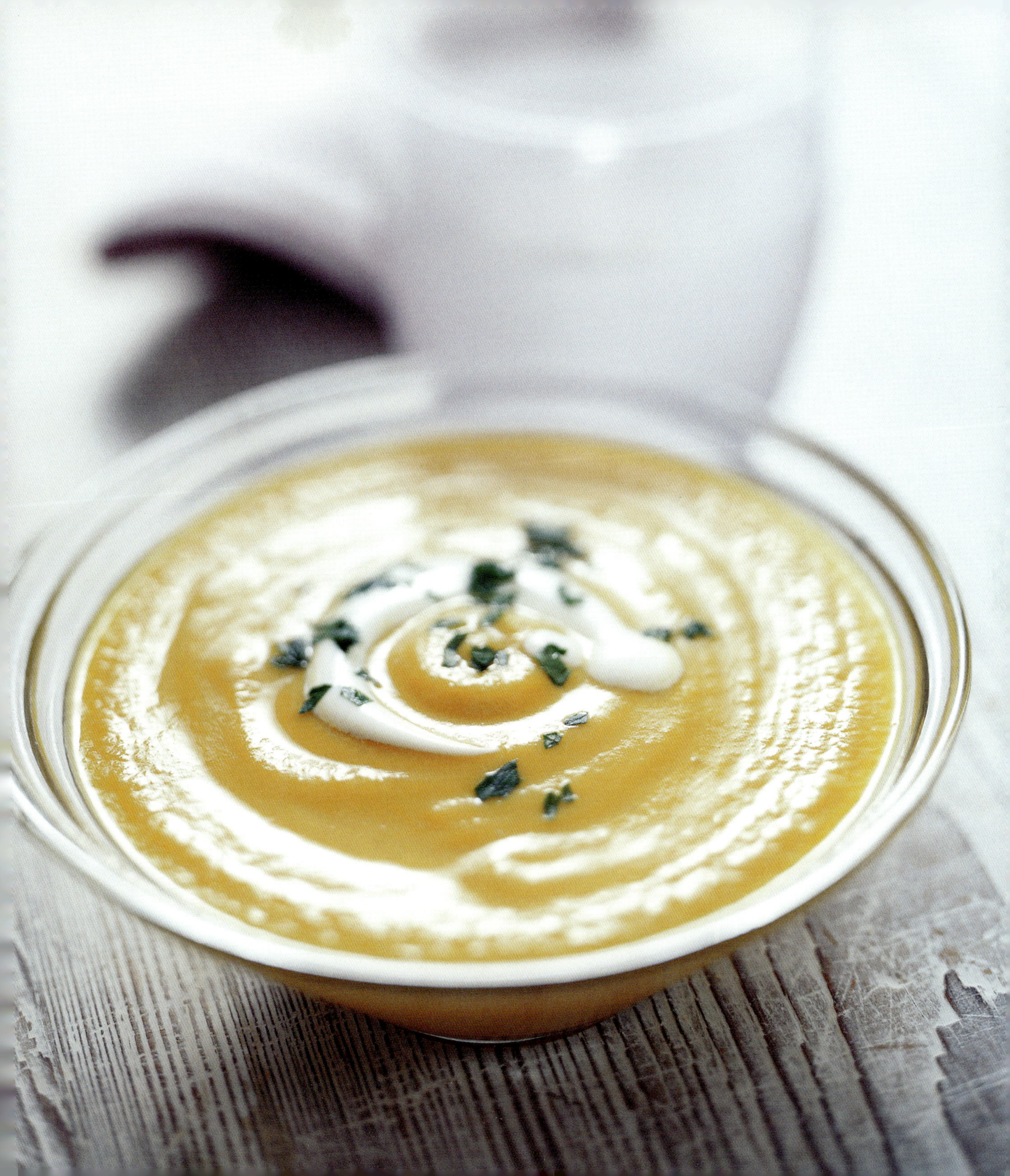

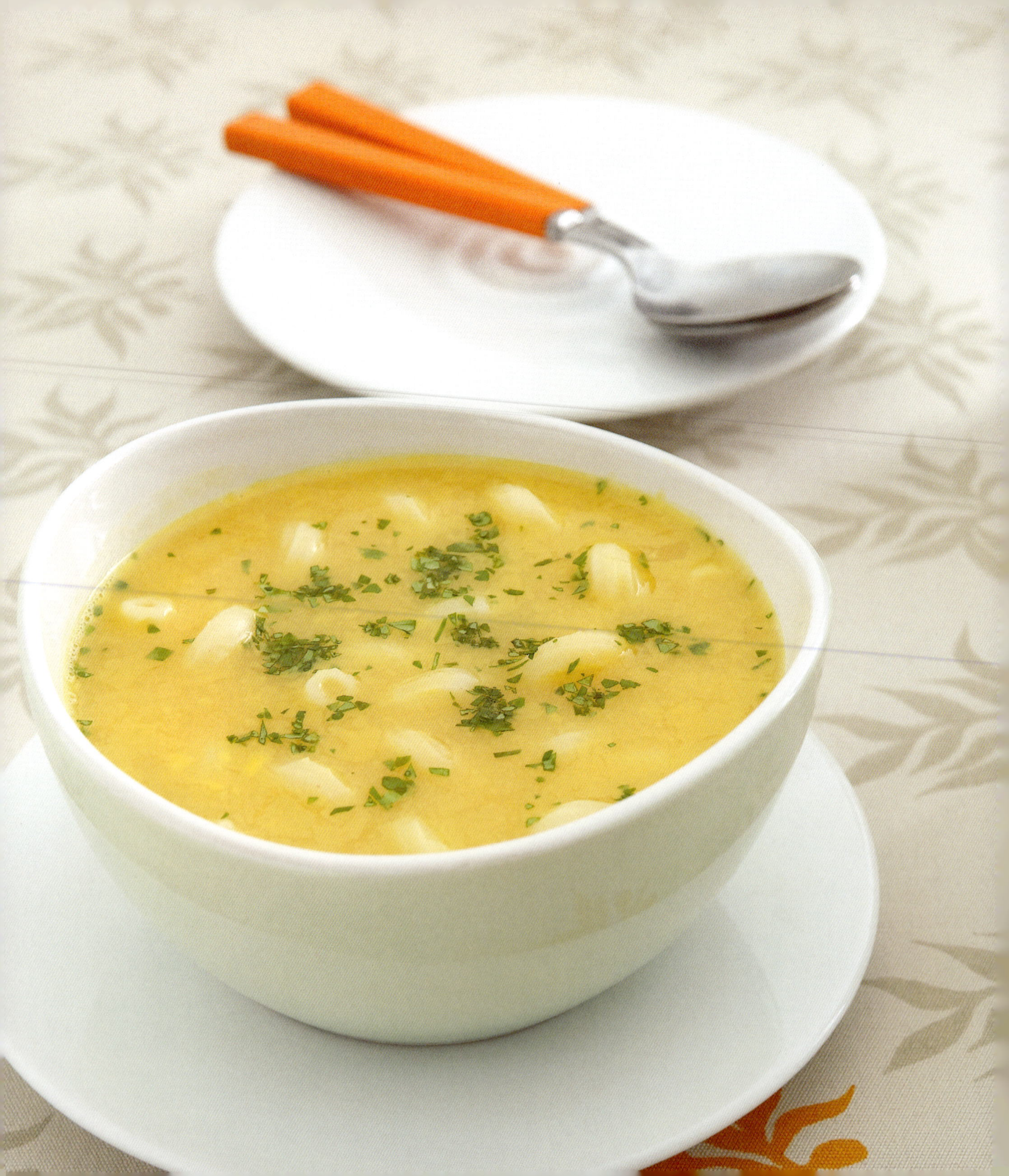

Carrot, lentil and pasta soup

1 tablespoon salt
1 tablespoon olive oil
1 carrot, roughly chopped
2 small onions, chopped
2 garlic cloves, crushed
½ tablespoon garam masala
200 g (7 oz) yellow lentils
2 litres/3½ pints/8 cups vegetable stock
100 g (3½ oz) small pasta
2 tablespoons fresh cilantro (coriander), chopped

serves 4

Heat the oil in a large pan set over a medium heat. Add the carrots, onions and garlic and cook, stirring occasionally, for 10 minutes or until the vegetables are soft. Add the garam masala and cook, stirring, for 1 minute longer.

Add the lentils and stock to the pan and bring to the boil. Reduce the heat and simmer, stirring occasionally, for 30–40 minutes, or until the lentils are cooked. Cool slightly.

Meanwhile, tip the pasta into a large pan of boiling salted water. Cook for 8 minutes, or until just firm in the centre (*al dente*). Drain, set aside and keep warm.

Purée the soup in batches, in a food processor or blender. Return the purée to a clean pan, add the pasta and cook over a low heat, stirring, for 5 minutes or until the soup is hot. Stir in the coriander and serve immediately.

Soups

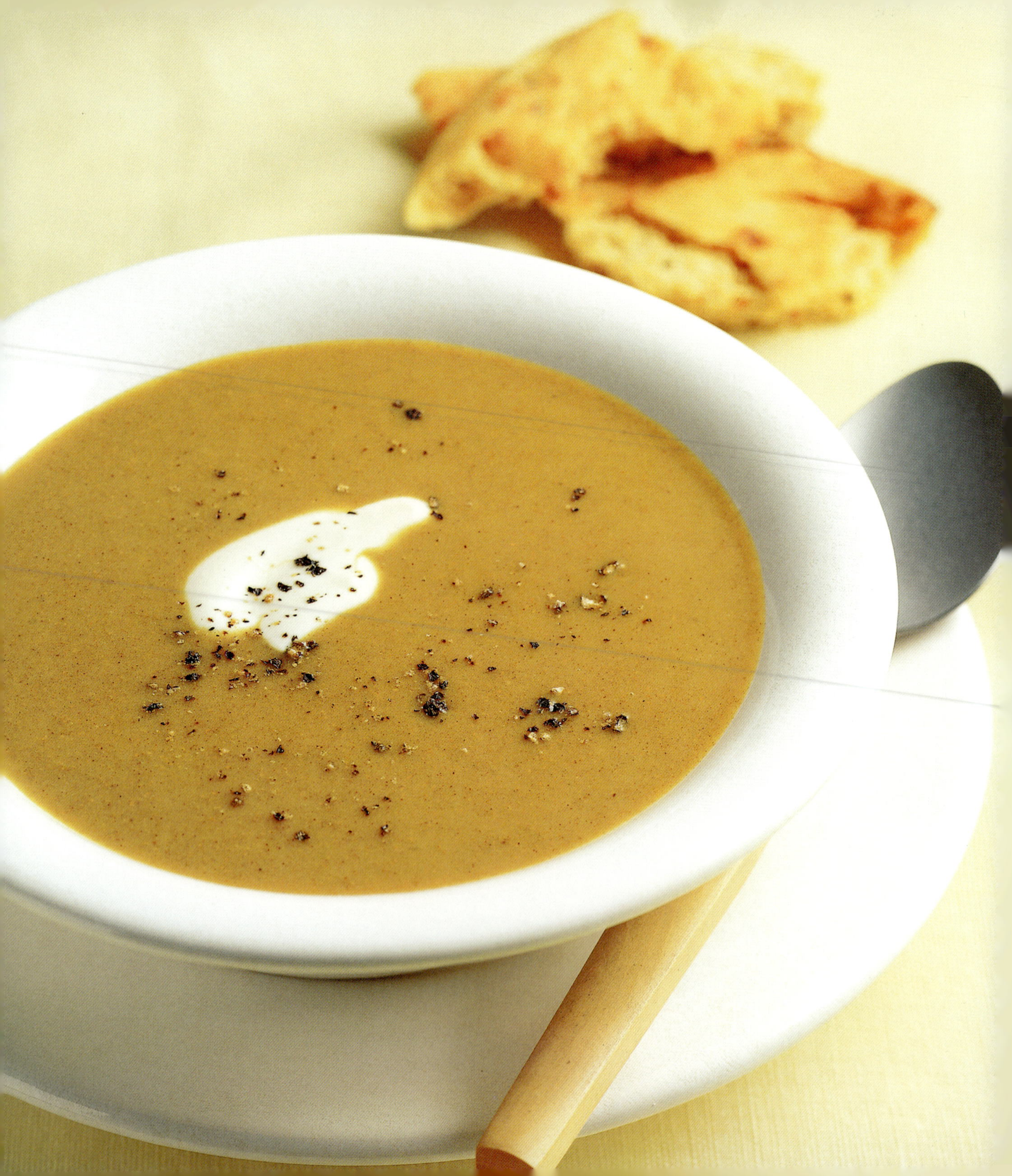

Spiced potato and onion soup

1 tablespoon vegetable oil
1 onion, finely chopped
1 cm/⅜ in piece root ginger, finely chopped
2 large potatoes, cut into 1 cm/⅜ in cubes
2 teaspoons ground cumin
2 teaspoons ground coriander
½ teaspoon turmeric
1 teaspoon ground cinnamon
1 litre/1¾ pints/4 cups vegetable stock
salt and freshly ground black pepper
1 tablespoons natural (plain) yogurt, to serve

Heat the oil in a large pan. Add the onion and ginger and fry for 5 minutes, or until softened. Add the potatoes and fry for another 1 minute, stirring often.

In a small bowl or cup, mix the cumin, coriander, turmeric and cinnamon with 2 tablespoons of cold water to make a paste. Add to the onion and potato mixture, stirring well, and fry for 1 minute to release the flavours.

Add the stock and season to taste. Bring to the boil, then reduce the heat, cover and simmer for 30 minutes, or until the potato is tender. Blend until smooth in a food processor. Return to the pan and gently heat through. Serve with a dollop of yogurt and more black pepper.

serves 4

Soups

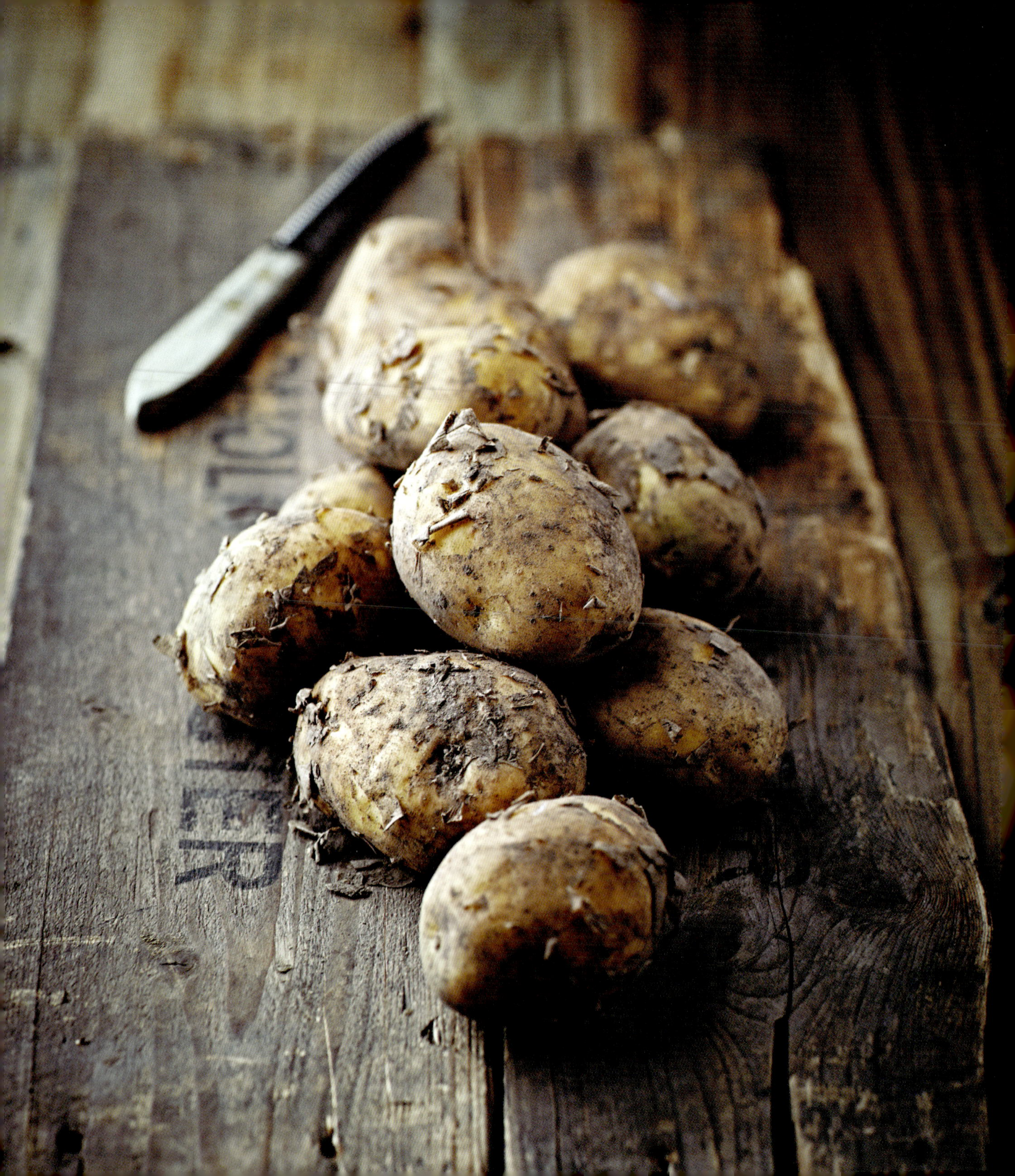

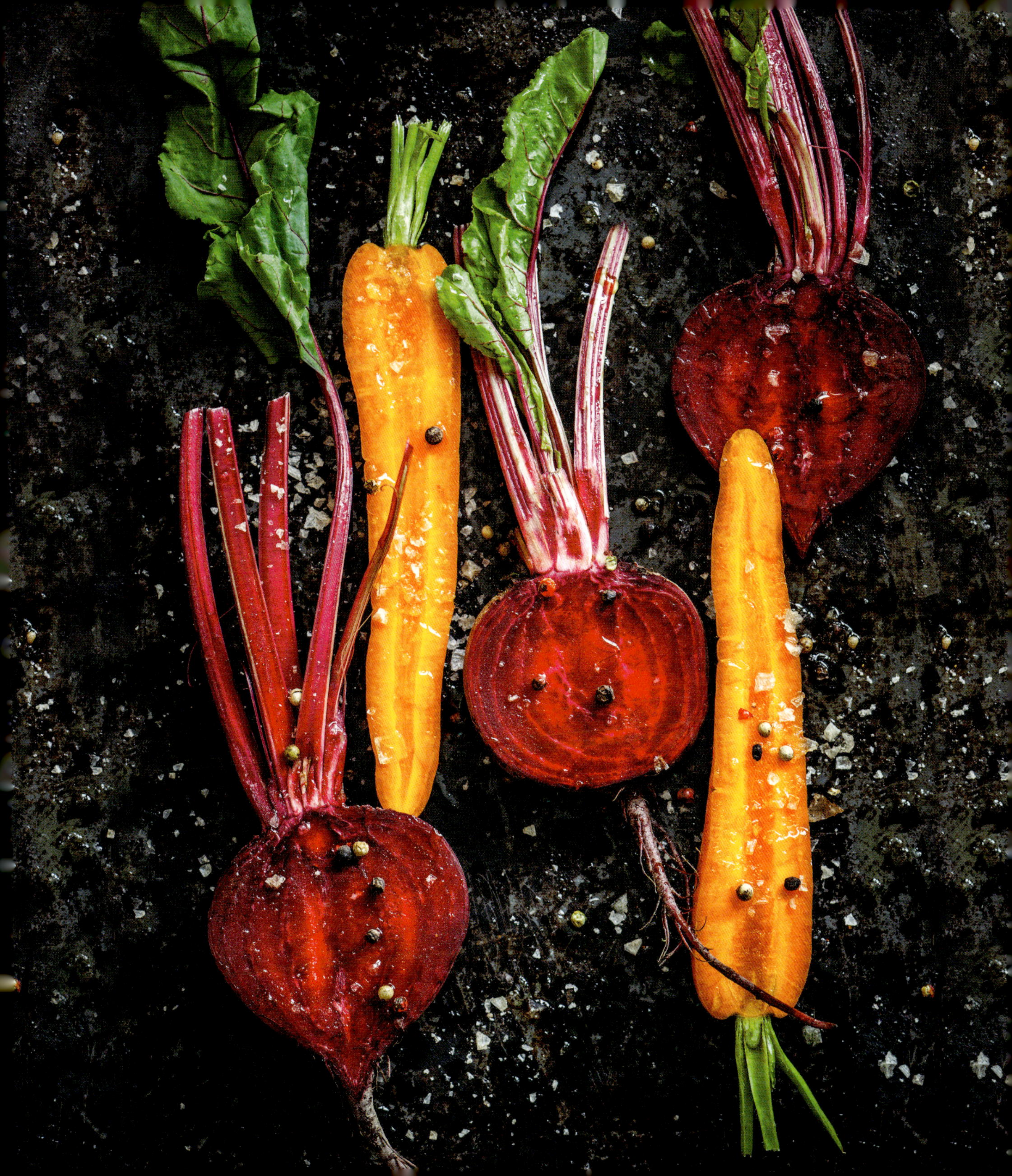

Swede and carrot soup

1 tablespoon oil
1 medium onion, diced
2 small carrots, peeled and chopped
1 swede, peeled and chopped
salt and freshly ground black pepper
250 ml/8 fl oz/1 cup vegetable stock
½ teaspoon ground ginger
¼ teaspoon ground nutmeg
500 ml/17 fl oz/2 cups fresh orange juice

In a large pan, heat the oil, then add the onion and sauté for 5 minutes, stirring occasionally.

Add the carrots, swede, salt and pepper. Sauté for 10 minutes, stirring occasionally.

Add the vegetable stock and cook, covered, over low heat for 20–30 minutes, until the vegetables are tender. Add the spices and stir through

Purée in the bowl of ta food processor with the orange juice. Reheat and serve.

serves 4

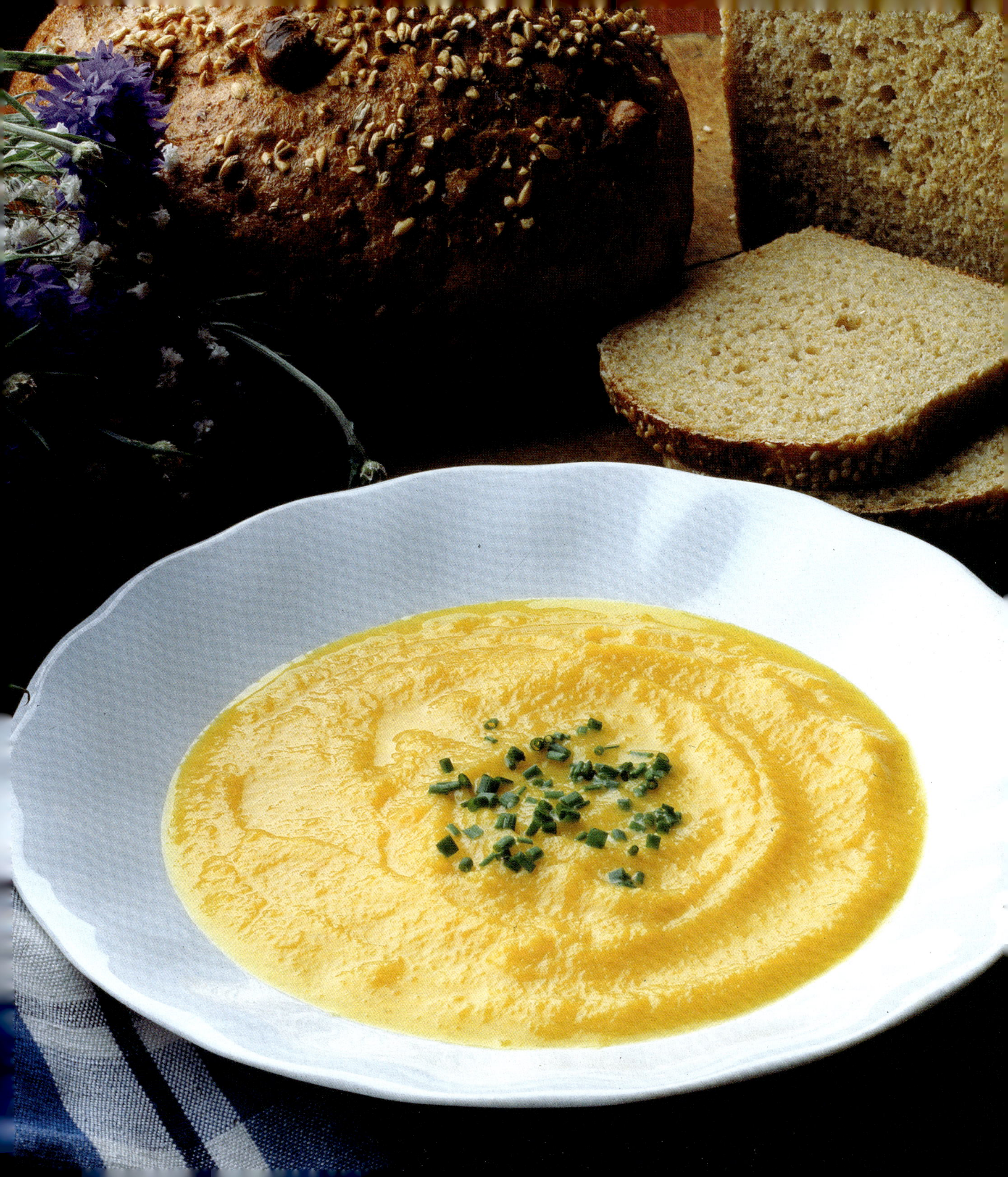

Curried cream of vegetable soup

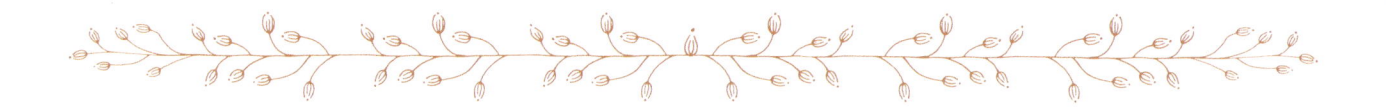

3 tablespoons vegetable oil
2 tablespoons curry powder
¼ teaspoon ground cinnamon
¼ teaspoon nutmeg
¼ teaspoon turmeric
¼ teaspoon ginger
3 carrots, diced
2 onions, chopped
2 garlic cloves, chopped
2 potatoes, diced
2 zucchini (courgettes), diced
1 litre/1¾ pints/4 cups vegetable stock
400 g/14 oz can cannellini beans, drained
220 g/8 oz can red kidney beans, drained
200 ml/7 fl oz crème fraîche
salt and freshly ground black pepper
2 teaspoons fresh flat-leaf parsley, chopped

Pour the oil into a large heavy pan and set over medium heat. Add the curry powder, cinnamon, nutmeg, turmeric and ginger and cook for 1 minute, then add the carrots, onions, garlic, potatoes and zucchini. Stir to coat thoroughly in the oil and spice mixture, and cook for another 5 minutes.

Add the stock and bring to the boil. Reduce the heat and simmer for 20 minutes, or until the vegetables are tender. Add the cannellini and red kidney beans and gently heat through. Remove from the heat and stir in the crème fraîche. Season to taste and serve sprinkled with the parsley.

serves 4

Soups

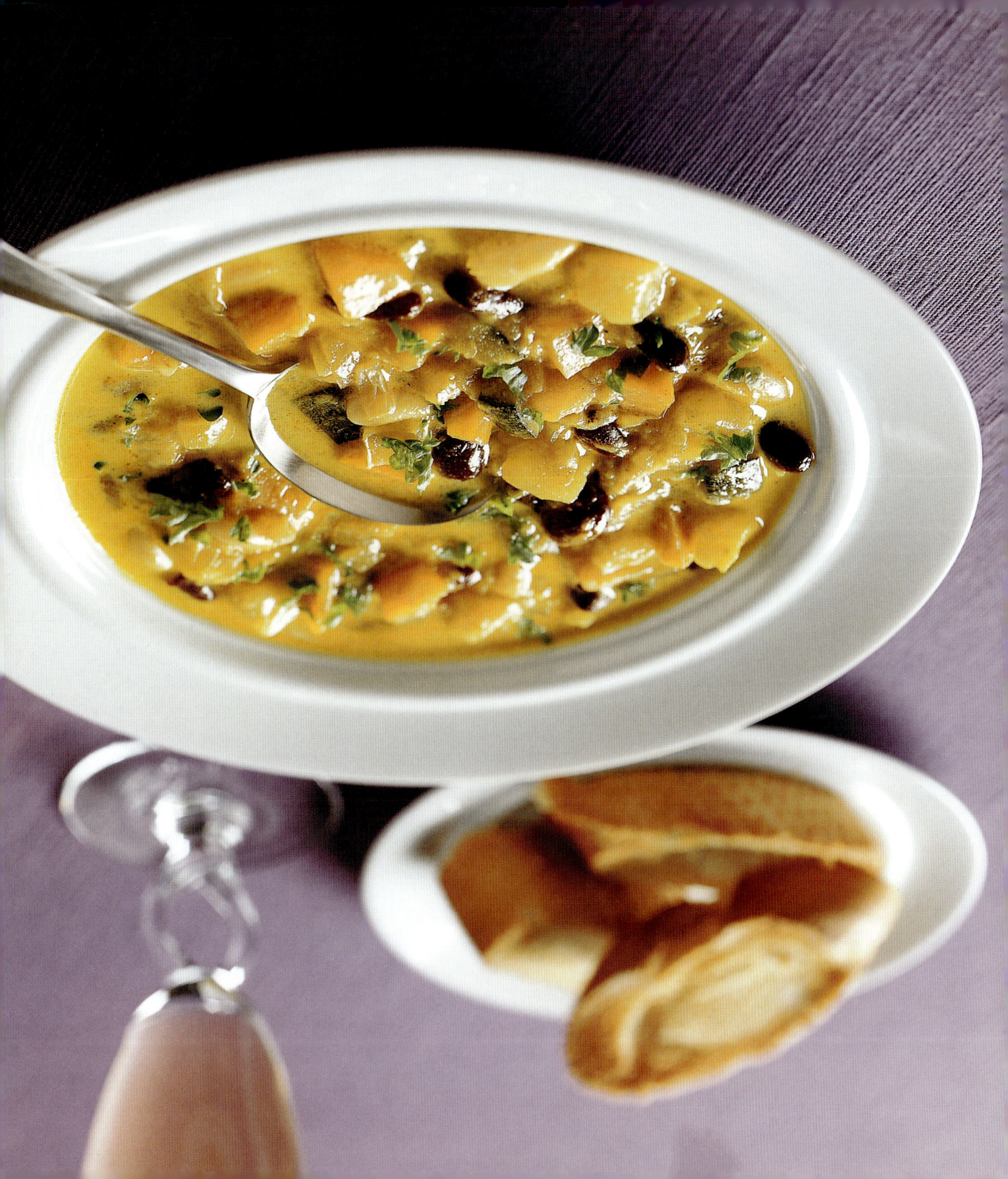

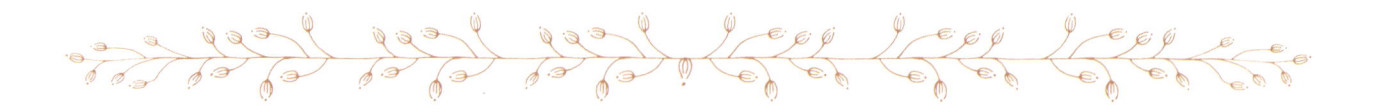

Lamb shank and vegetable soup

serves 6

4 lamb shanks, French trimmed
3 celery stalks, cut into 1 cm/3/8 in pieces
2 medium carrots, peeled and cut into 1 cm/3/8 in pieces
1 swede, peeled and cut into 1 cm/3/8 in cubes
1 parsnip, peeled and cut into 1 cm/3/8 in cubes
2 x 400 g/14 oz cans tomato soup
1/3 cup/3 tablespoons flat-leaf parsley, coarsely chopped
salt and freshly ground black pepper
crusty bread, to serve

Combine the lamb shanks, celery, carrot, swede, parsnip, tomato soup and 1.5 litres/2¾ pints/6 cups cold water in a large pan set over high heat, and bring to the boil. Reduce the heat to low and simmer, covered, stirring occasionally, for 2¼ hours or until the lamb is tender and falling away from the bone.

Remove from the heat and stir in the parsley. Use tongs to remove the bones. Taste and season with salt and pepper. Ladle soup into bowls and serve with crusty bread.

Sweet potato, pasta and leek soup

serves 6

2 teaspoons canola oil
2 leeks, thinly sliced
pinch of saffron threads
1 kg/2¼ lb sweet potato, peeled and chopped
2 litres/3½ pints/8 cups chicken stock
1 cinnamon stick
1 bouquet garni
125 g/4½ oz tiny pasta pieces for soup
2 tablespoons fresh chives, chopped

FOR THE LAVASH CRISPS
2 sheets lavash bread
1 tablespoon olive oil
2 tablespoons Parmesan, finely grated

Heat the oil in a large pot set over medium heat. Add the leeks and cook for 5 minutes, or until the leeks are soft and golden. Add the saffron and sweet potato and stir for about 5 minutes, or until the sweet potato begins to soften.

Stir in the stock, cinnamon stick and bouquet garni. Bring to the boil, then reduce the heat and simmer for 30 minutes, or until the sweet potato is very soft. Remove the cinnamon stick and bouquet garni.

Cook the pasta in a large stockpot of rapidly boiling water until al dente. Drain well.

Purée the soup in batches until smooth, then return to the pan along with the pasta and reheat gently. If it is too thick add a little water.

For the lavash crisps, use a star-shaped cookie cutter to stamp out shapes from the bread. Brush them lightly with oil, scatter with Parmesan and stack another star on top. Grill (broil) until crisp and golden.

To serve, ladle the soup into bowls, float lavash stars on top and sprinkle with chives.

Soups

51

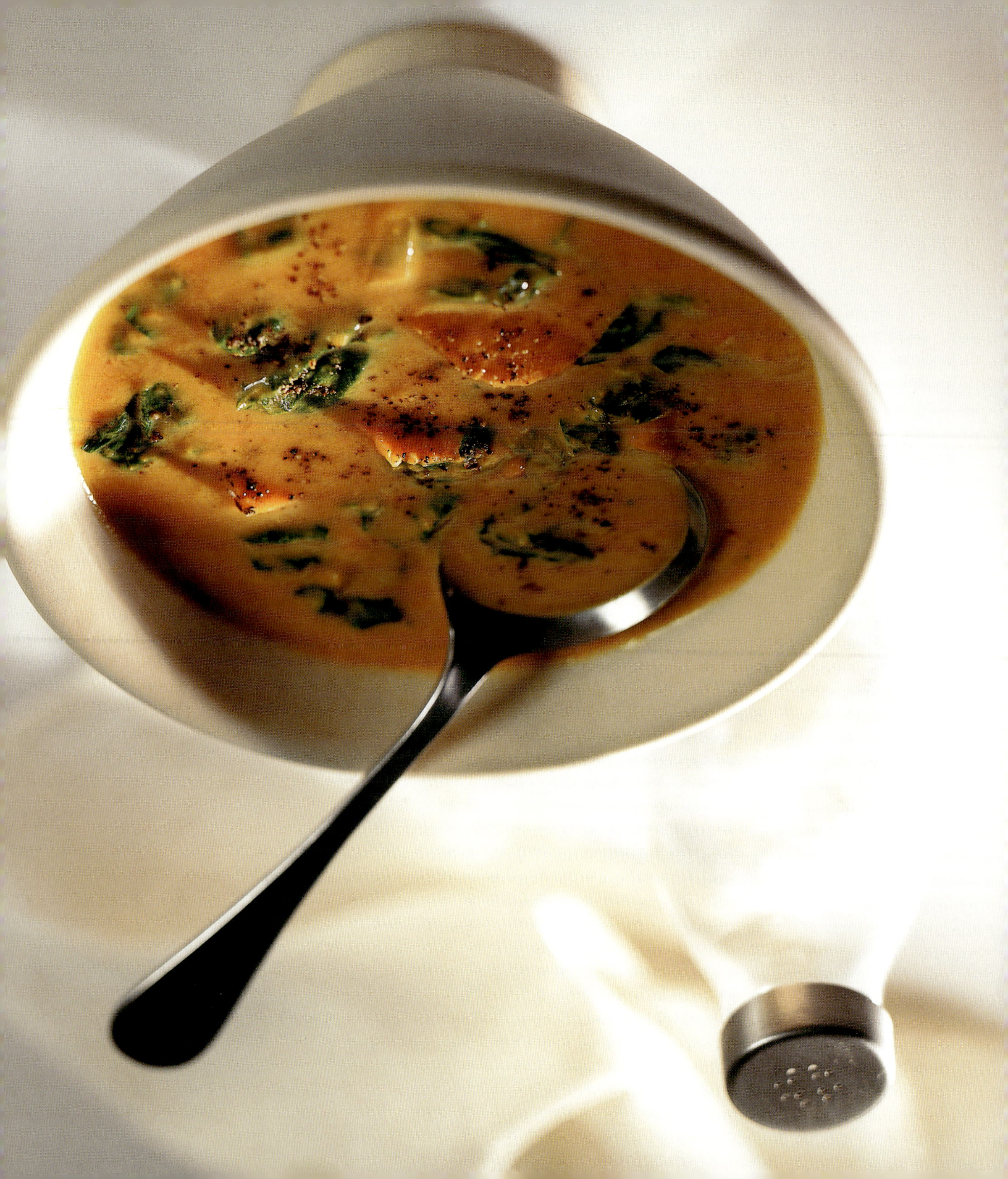

Coconut, sweet potato and spinach soup

25 g/¾ oz butter
450 g/1 lb sweet potatoes, cut into 1 cm/⅜ in dice
1 onion, chopped
2 garlic cloves, crushed
1 teaspoon grated root ginger
1 tablespoon medium curry paste
600 ml/1 pint vegetable stock
200 ml/7 fl oz coconut milk
juice of 1 lime
¼ teaspoon dried crushed chillies
175 g/6 oz fresh spinach, shredded
salt and freshly ground black pepper

Melt the butter in a large pan set over medium heat. Add the potatoes, onion, garlic, ginger and curry paste and fry for 5 minutes, or until lightly golden.

Add the stock, coconut milk, lime juice and chilli. Bring to the boil, cover and simmer for 15 minutes, or until the potatoes are tender.

Leave the soup to cool a little, then purée half of it with a hand blender. Return the purée to the pan, add the spinach and cook for 1–2 minutes, until the spinach has just wilted and the soup has heated through. Season to taste.

serves 4

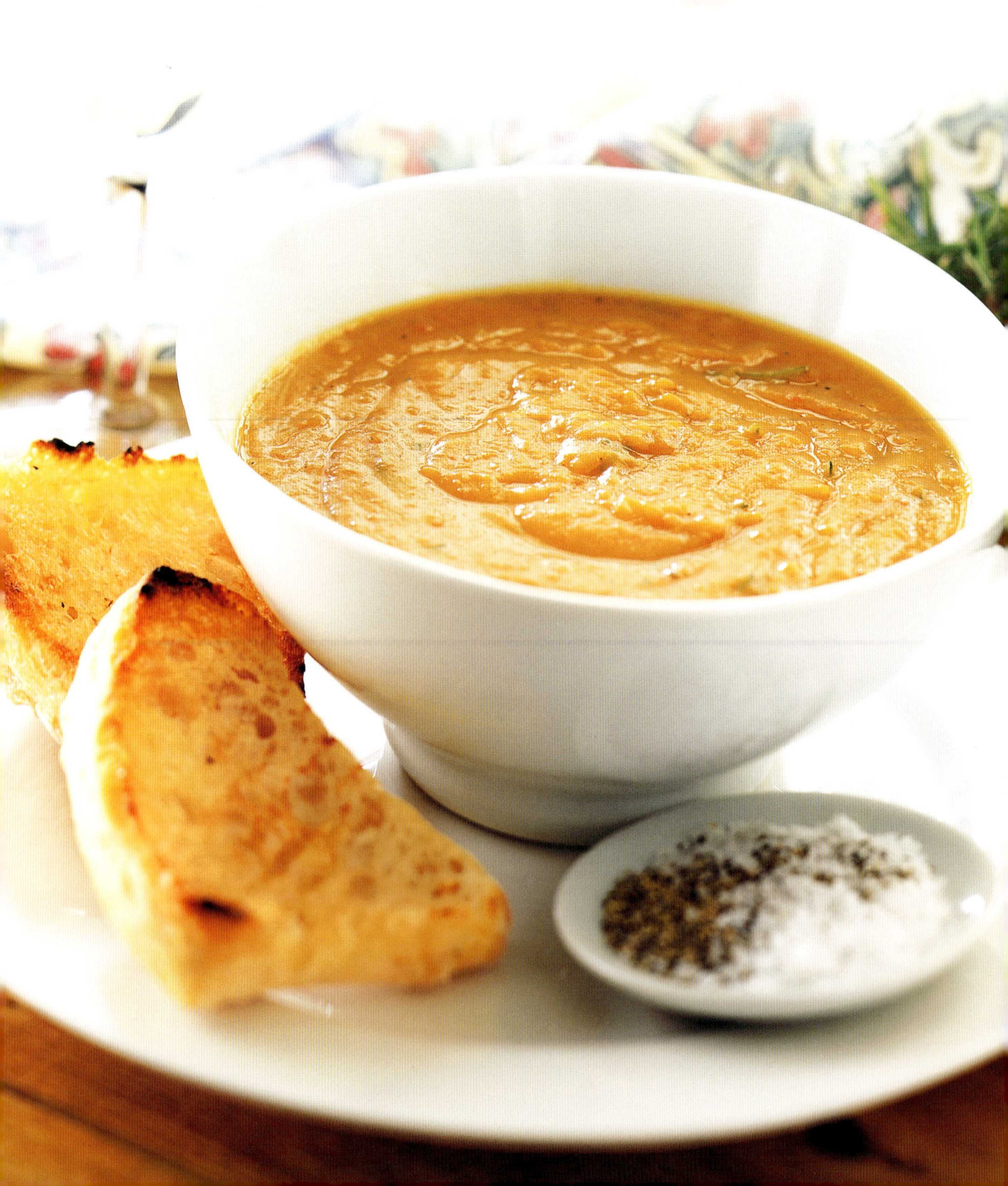

Sweet potato and rosemary soup

2 tablespoons olive oil
2 garlic cloves, crushed
1 medium onion, chopped
3 tablespoons chopped fresh rosemary
2 tablespoons puréed semi-dried tomato
1 medium carrot, sliced
1 large potato, sliced
700 g/1½ lb sweet potato, sliced
1 litre/1¾ pints/4 cups chicken stock
salt and freshly ground black pepper

serves 4–6

Heat the oil in a large pan. Add the garlic, onion and one-third of the rosemary, and cook over a medium heat for 5 minutes. Add the semi-dried tomato purée and cook for 1 minute.

Add the carrots, potatoes and sweet potato, and cook for another 6 minutes.

Transfer to a slow cooker set on high and add the stock and salt and pepper. Cook for 5 hours, or until the vegetables are soft.

Purée the soup in a food processor, then return to the slow cooker. Add the remaining rosemary and heat through before serving.

Soups

Entrées

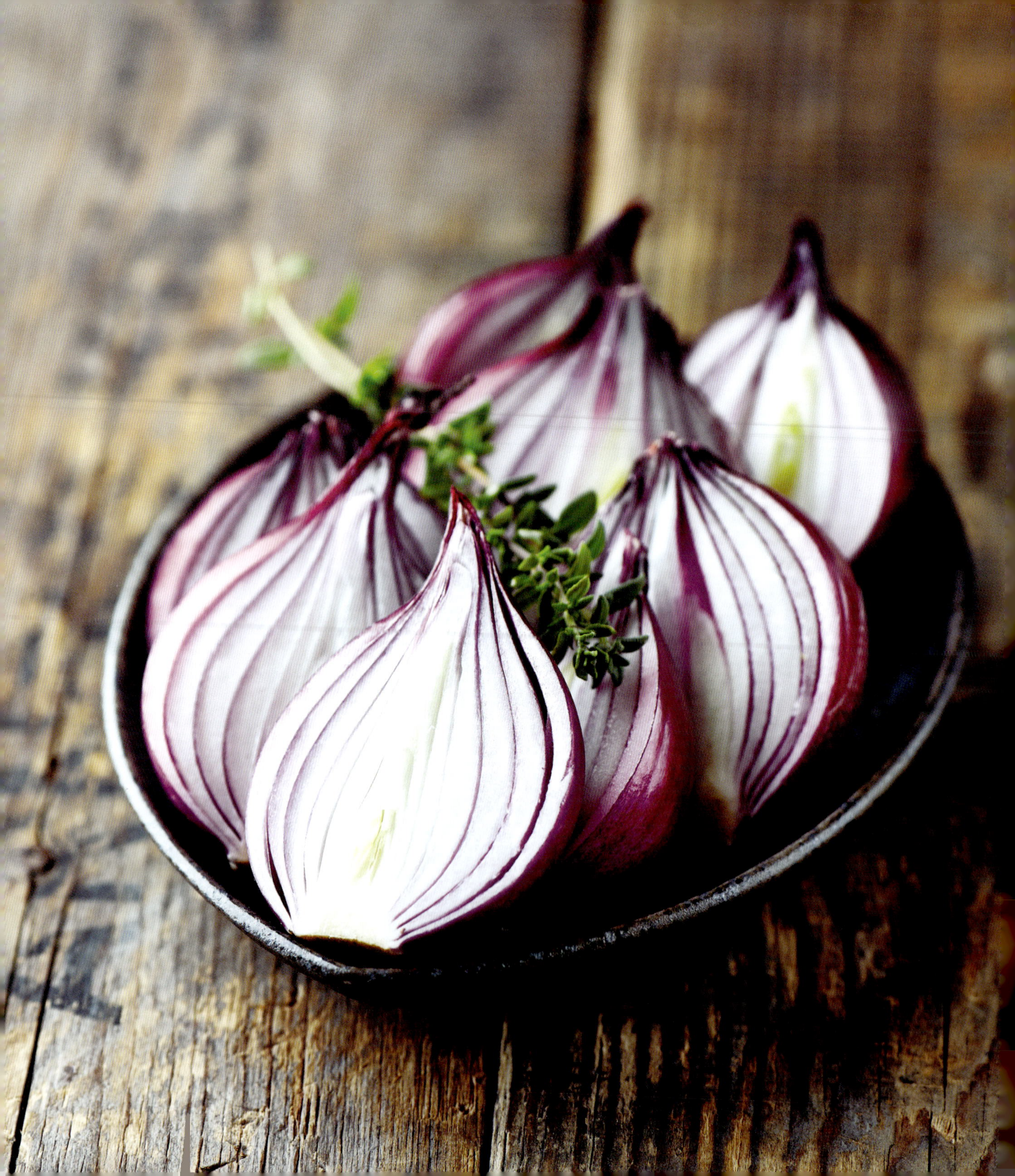

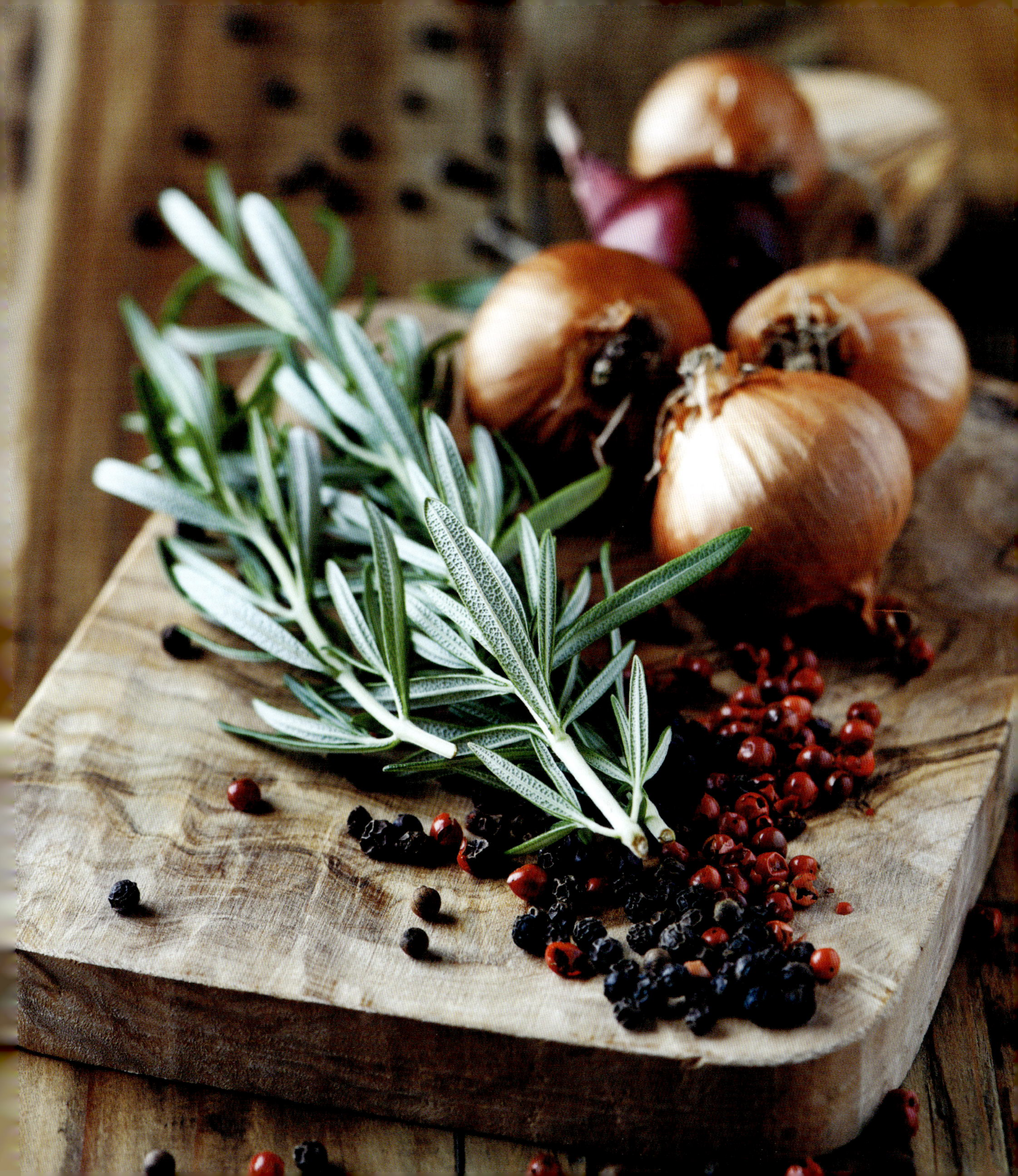

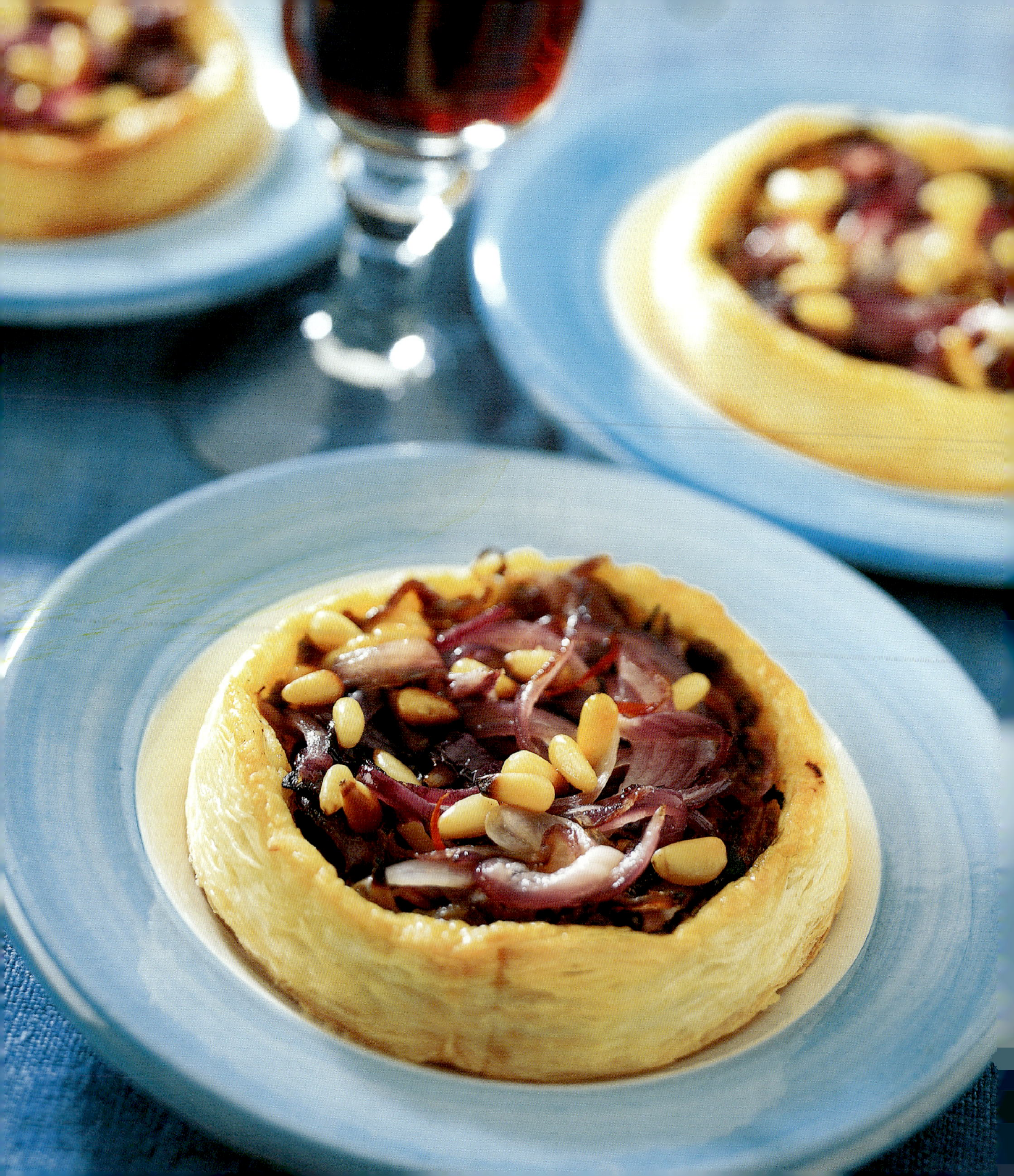

Red onion and chilli tarts

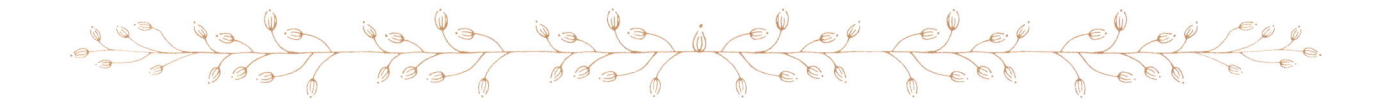

375 g/13 oz ready-rolled puff pastry
1 tablespoon olive oil
200 g/7 oz red onions, halved and finely sliced lengthwise
1 small red chilli, deseeded and thinly sliced
2 tablespoons red pesto
25 g/¾ oz pine nuts

serves 4

Preheat the oven to 220°C/425°F/Gas mark 7.

Open out the pastry sheet and stamp out four 12 cm/4¾ in rounds. Use a slightly smaller cutter or a sharp knife to score a border 1 cm/³/₈ in from the edge of each – this will form the rim. Place the rounds on a baking sheet.

Heat the oil in a large frying pan. Fry the onions for 10 minutes or until softened, stirring. Add the chilli and cook gently for 1 minute, then season.

Spread the pesto over the pastry rounds, leaving the rim clear. Spoon the onion mixture over the pesto and scatter with the pine nuts. Cook for 12–15 minutes, until the pastry has risen and is golden brown.

Entrées

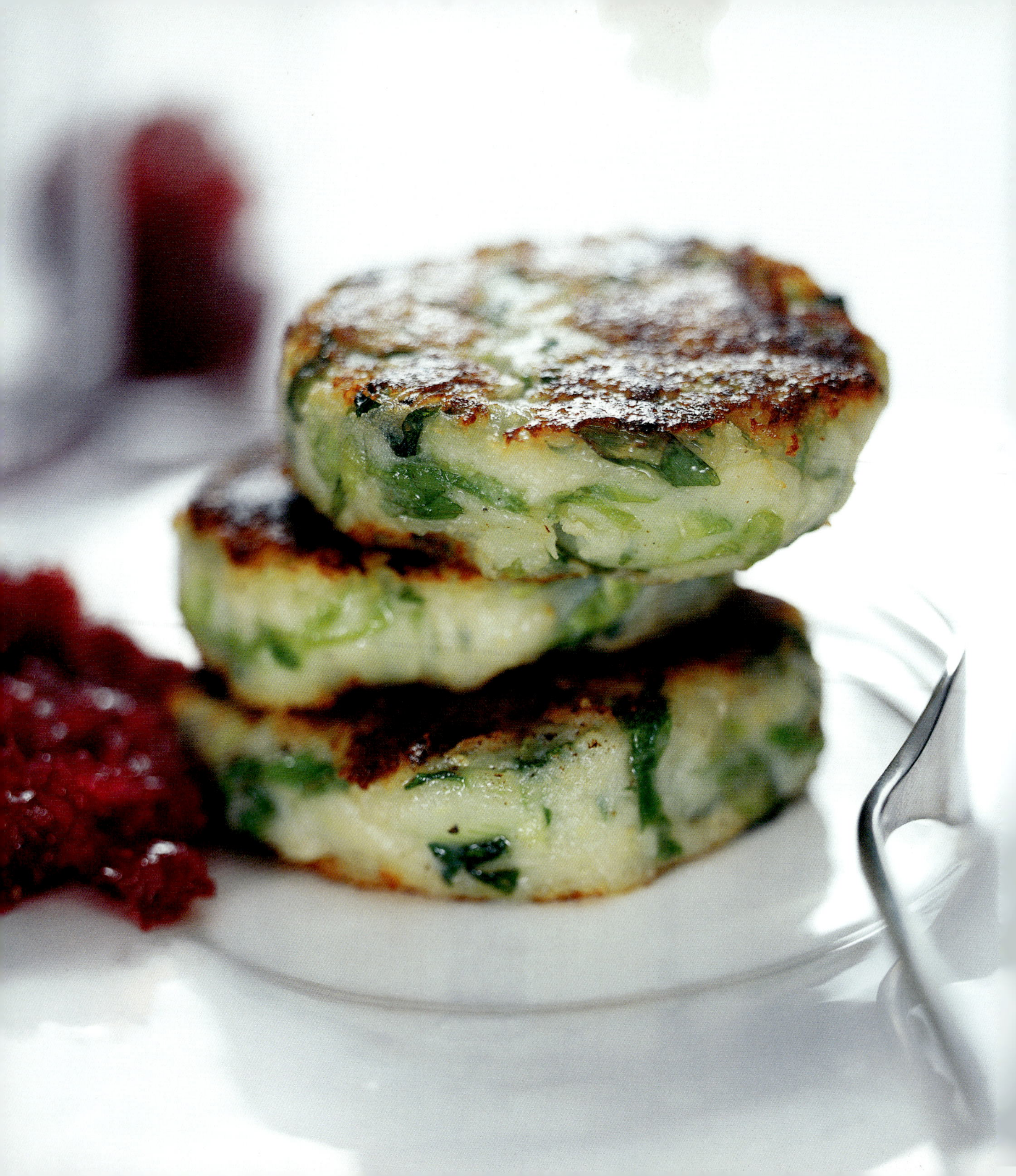

Bubble and squeak with onion chutney

675 g/1 lb 7 oz potatoes, peeled and cut into even-sized pieces
1 garlic clove, peeled
125 g/4½ oz Savoy cabbage, finely shredded
4 spring onions (scallions), finely sliced
salt and freshly ground black pepper
25 g/¾ oz butter
1 tablespoon sunflower oil

FOR THE ONION CHUTNEY
2 large or 6 small red onions, finely chopped
50 g/1¾ oz brown sugar
1 tablespoon white wine vinegar

Place the potatoes and garlic in a large pan and cover with water. Bring to the boil, cover and simmer for 15–20 minutes, until tender. Drain, return to the pan and mash until smooth. Cool.

Meanwhile, place the cabbage in a pan and pour over boiling water to just cover, bring back to the boil, then drain. Add the cabbage, spring onions and seasoning to the potato and mix well.

Place all the ingredients for the chutney in a saucepan and bring to the boil over a low heat. Simmer gently, uncovered, for about 20 minutes, or until almost all of the liquid has evaporated.

Divide the potato into eight and shape into flat rounds. Melt the butter and oil in a frying pan and fry the cakes over a medium heat for 5 minutes on one side. Turn over, taking care as the cakes are quite soft, and cook for another 5 minutes, until golden and heated through. Serve with the chutney.

serves 4

Entrées

Potato rösti with smoked trout

400 g/14 oz sebago potatoes, washed
45 g/1½ oz butter, melted
50 g/1¾ oz/ watercress
½ smoked trout, bones and skin removed

serves 2

Place the unpeeled potatoes in a medium saucepan. Cover with cold water and bring to the boil. Cook for 10 minutes, drain and allow to cool completely. Peel and grate the potatoes and place in a medium bowl. Add the melted butter and toss to combine.

Preheat a large non-stick frying pan over medium-high heat. Place two mounds of potato onto the pan and flatten with a spatula. Cook for 10 minutes on both sides, or until golden brown and crisp. Place rthe östis onto two serving plates. Top with watercress and smoked trout.

Entrées

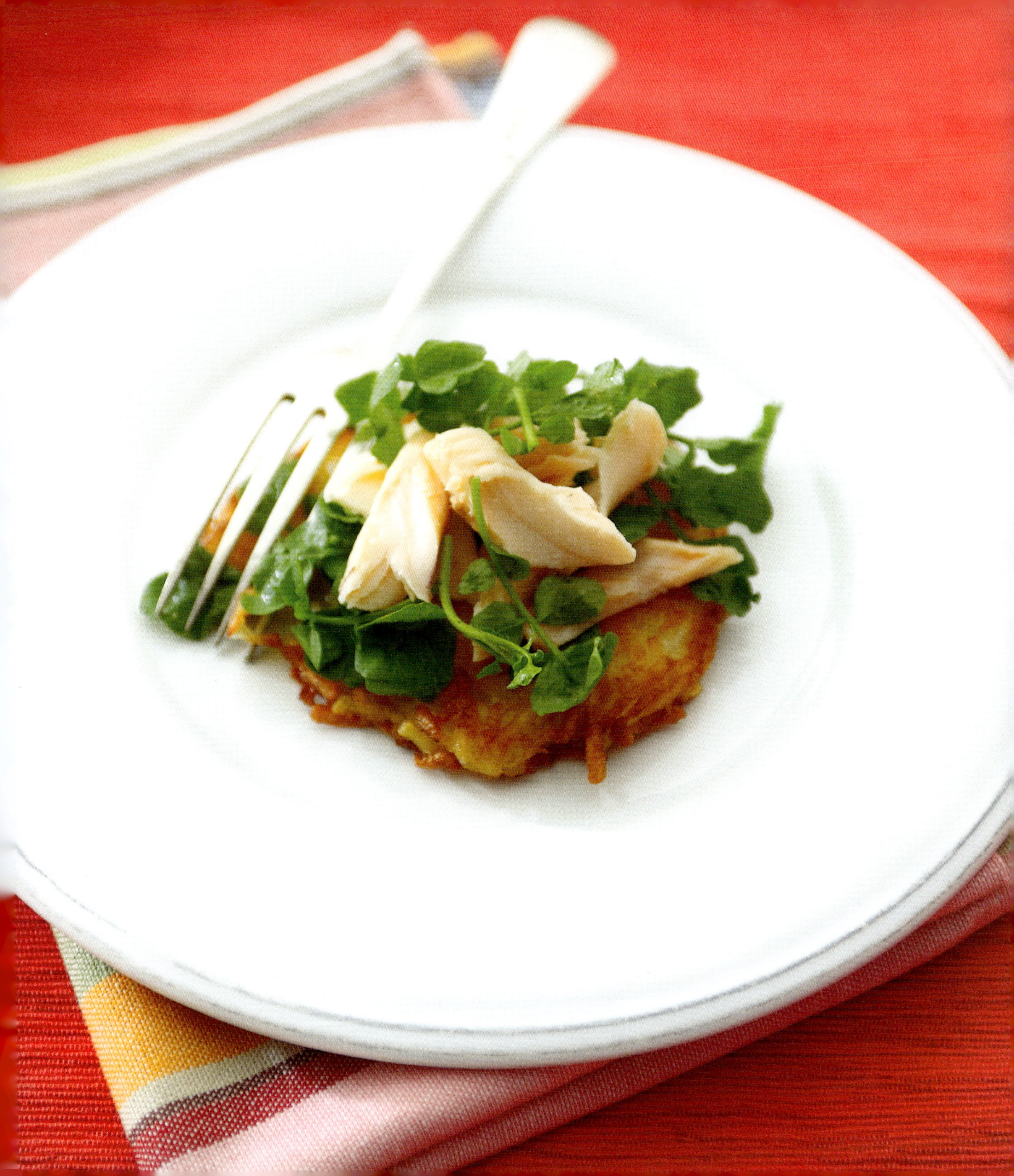

Individual sweet potato quiche

2 sheets shortcrust pastry, thawed
1 tablespoon olive oil
2 teaspoons butter
1 large brown onion, halved and thinly sliced
1 sweet potato, about 300 g/10 oz/, peeled and cut into 2.5 cm/1 in pieces
175 ml/6 fl oz/¾ cup thickened (heavy, double) cream
3 eggs, lightly whisked
¼ cup/2 tablespoons basil, chopped

makes 12

Stamp out circles from the pastry and press into a 12-cup muffin tray. Refrigerate for 15 minutes.

Heat the oil and butter in a frying pan over medium heat. Add the onion and cook, stirring occasionally, for 15 minutes until the onion caramelises.

Meanwhile, cook the sweet potato in a medium pan of boiling water for 5 minutes, or until tender. Drain well.

Preheat the oven to 200°C/400°F/Gas mark 6. Prick the pastry lightly with a fork, then line with baking paper. Half-fill with rice and bake for 10 minutes, or until lightly browned. Discard the rice and paper. Reduce the oven temperature to 180°C/350°F/Gas mark 4.

Cover the pastry bases with caramelised onion and top with sweet potato. Whisk together the cream, eggs and basil in a bowl, then ladle into the pastry bases. Bake for 15 minutes, or until golden and set.

Entrées

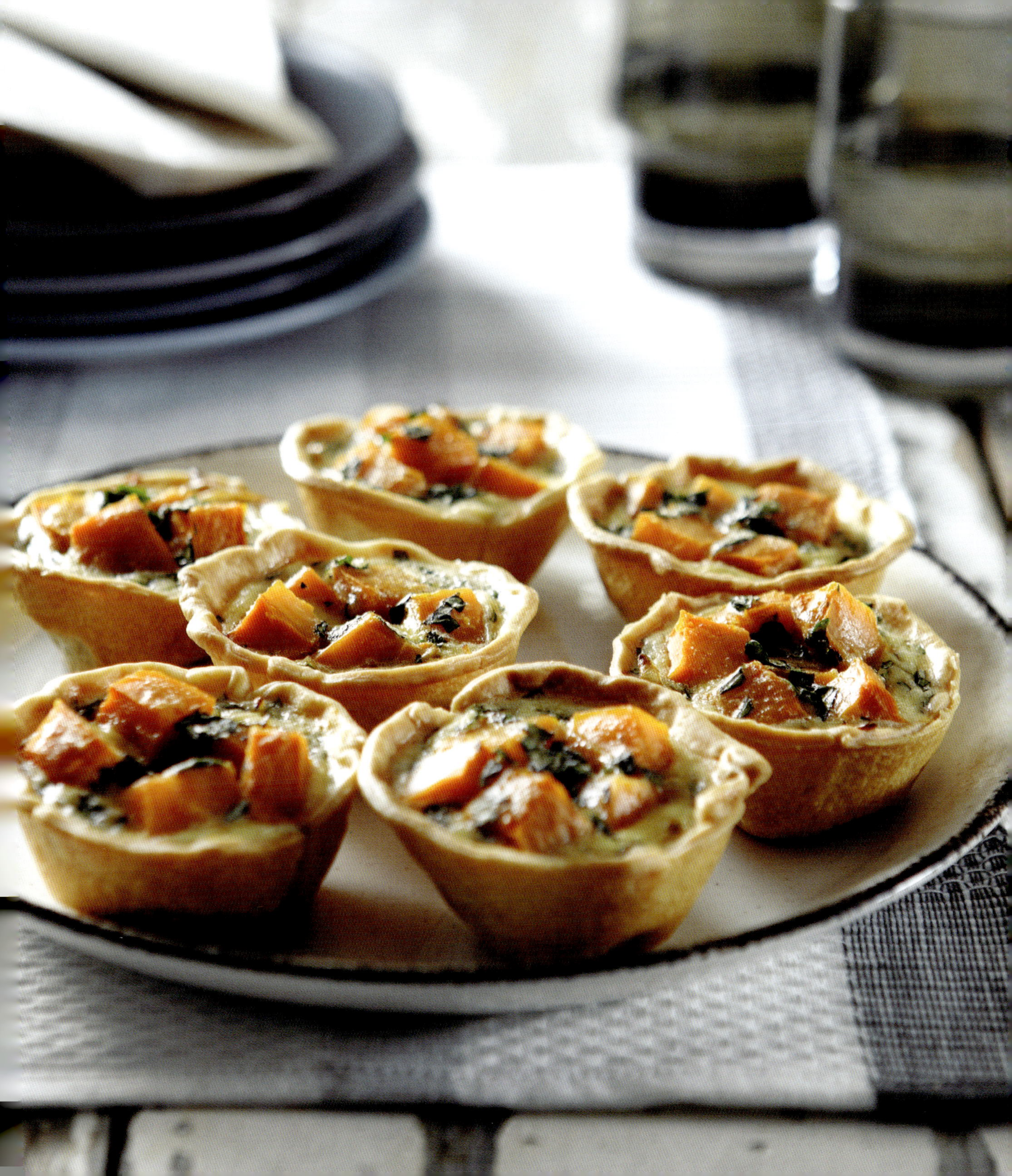

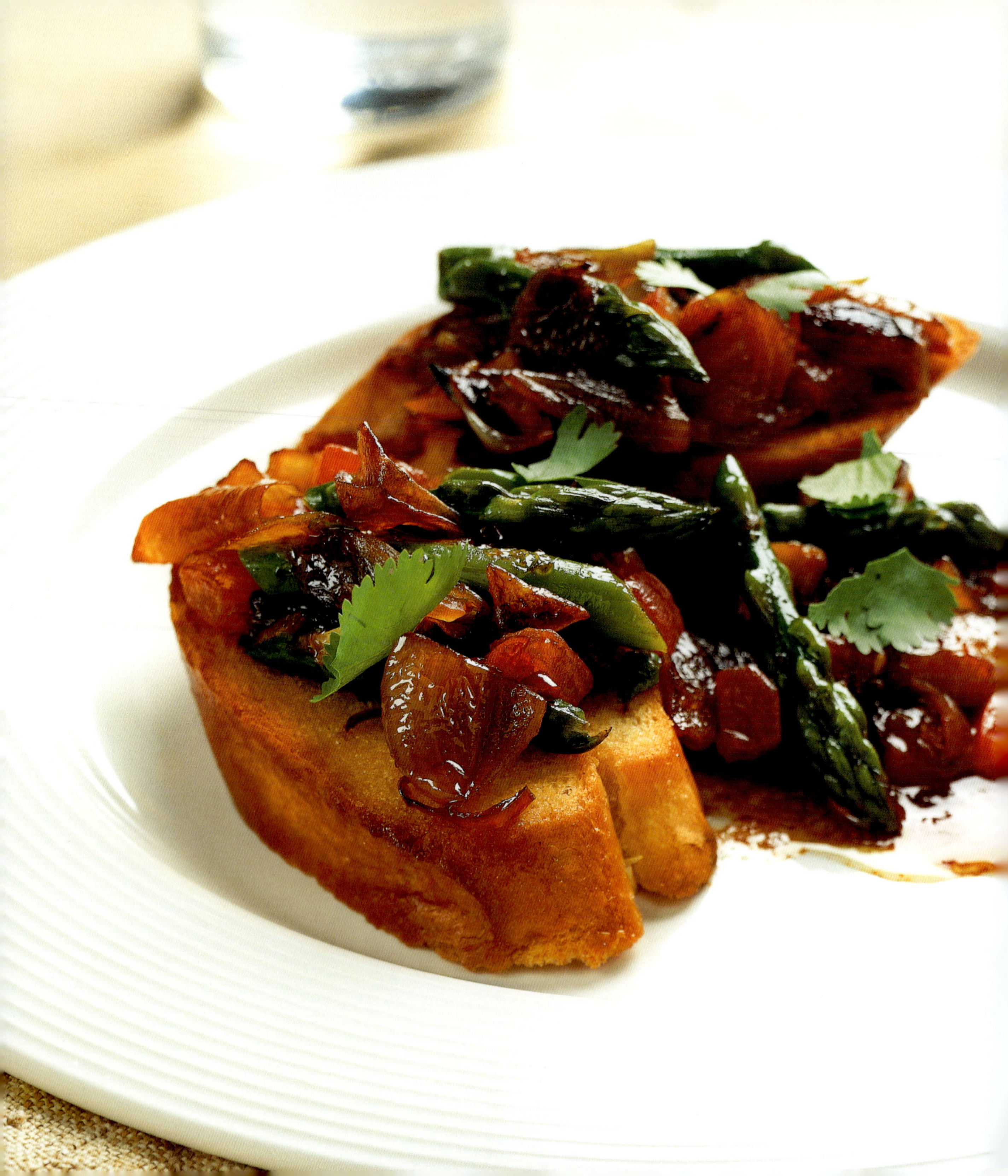

Caramelised shallot and asparagus toasts

60 ml/2 fl oz/¼ cup olive oil

300 g/10½ oz French shallots, roughly chopped

2 garlic cloves, thickly sliced

1 red chilli, deseeded and sliced (optional)

1½ tablespoons soft dark brown sugar

2 tablespoons dark soy sauce

1 tablespoon white wine vinegar or cider vinegar

150 ml/5 fl oz/ white wine

handful of asparagus, tips only

4 Roma tomatoes

juice of 1½ lemon

2 medium baguettes, thickly sliced

flat-leaf parsley or coriander (cilantro), to garnish

Heat the oil in a wok or large heavy frying pan. Add the shallots, garlic and chilli (if using) and stir-fry for 4–5 minutes, until they start to colour. Add the sugar and the soy sauce and stir-fry for 3–4 minutes, until the shallots are evenly browned.

Add the vinegar and wine to the shallots and bring to the boil. Reduce the heat and simmer, uncovered, for 8 minutes, or until the shallots have softened and the liquid has thickened and looks glossy. Add the asparagus tips, cover and cook for 4–5 minutes, stirring occasionally.

Cut a cross in the base of each tomato. Place the tomatoes in a bowl and cover with boiling water. Leave for 30 seconds, then peel, deseed and chop. Add to the pan with the lemon juice, stir and heat for 1–2 minutes.

Meanwhile, heat the grill (broiler) to high. Toast the bread on both sides. Serve the toasts topped with the vegetable mixture and garnished with the parsley or coriander.

serves 6

Entrées

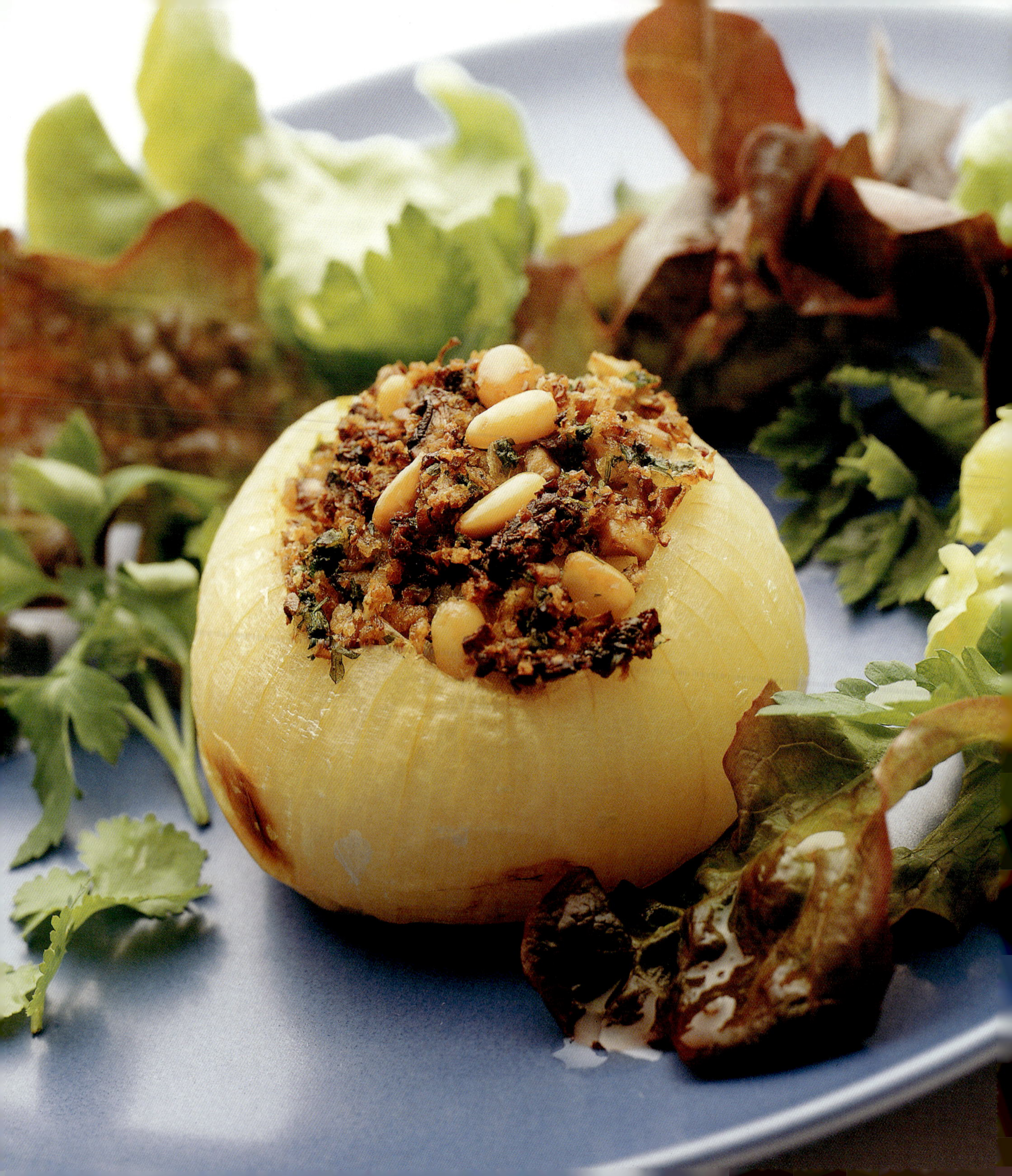

Baked onions with mushrooms and pine nuts

2 slices brown bread
4 large onions
2 tablespoons olive oil
2 garlic cloves, chopped
2 tablespoons pine nuts
200 g/7 oz mushrooms, finely chopped
1/3 cup/3 tablespoons fresh parsley, chopped
salt and freshly ground black pepper

serves 4

Preheat the oven to 160°C/325°F/Gas mark 3. Place the bread in the oven for 20 minutes, or until it becomes crisp. Process in a food processor to make breadcrumbs.

Slice the tops and bases off the onions and discard them. Place the onions in a saucepan, cover with water and bring to the boil. Cook for 10 minutes to soften. Drain, then leave to cool for 20 minutes.

Increase the oven temperature to 200°C/400°F/Gas mark 6. Remove the centre of the onion and finely chop it.

In a large frying pan heat the oil and cook the garlic and chopped onion for 5 minutes. Add the pine nuts and mushrooms and cook for another 5 minutes. Remove from the heat and mix in the breadcrumbs, parsley and seasoning.

Fill the onion shells with the mixture, then wrap each onion in foil, leaving the tops open. Place on a baking sheet and bake for 40 minutes or until the onions are tender.

Entrées

Chilli bean potatoes

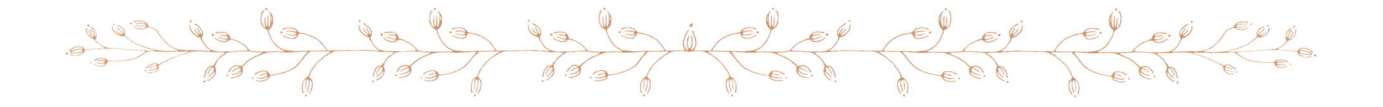

4 potatoes, scrubbed
3 large red chillies
1 tablespoon tomato paste
½ teaspoon paprika
315g/11oz can red kidney beans, drained and rinsed
freshly ground black pepper
115 g/4 oz/½ cup Cheddar (tasty) cheese, grated

serves 4

Preheat the oven to 220°C/425°F/Gas mark 7. Bake the potatoes and chillies for 50 minutes until the potatoes are soft. Remove from oven and allow to cool slightly. Remove the skins and seeds from the chillies, then set aside.

Cut a cross in the tops of the potatoes and scoop out the flesh, leaving a thin shell. Place the potato flesh, tomato paste, paprika and roasted chilli in a bowl and mash. Stir in the beans and season to taste with black pepper.

Spoon the mixture into the potato shells, top with cheese, and bake for 10–15 minutes, or until heated through and lightly browned.

Entrées

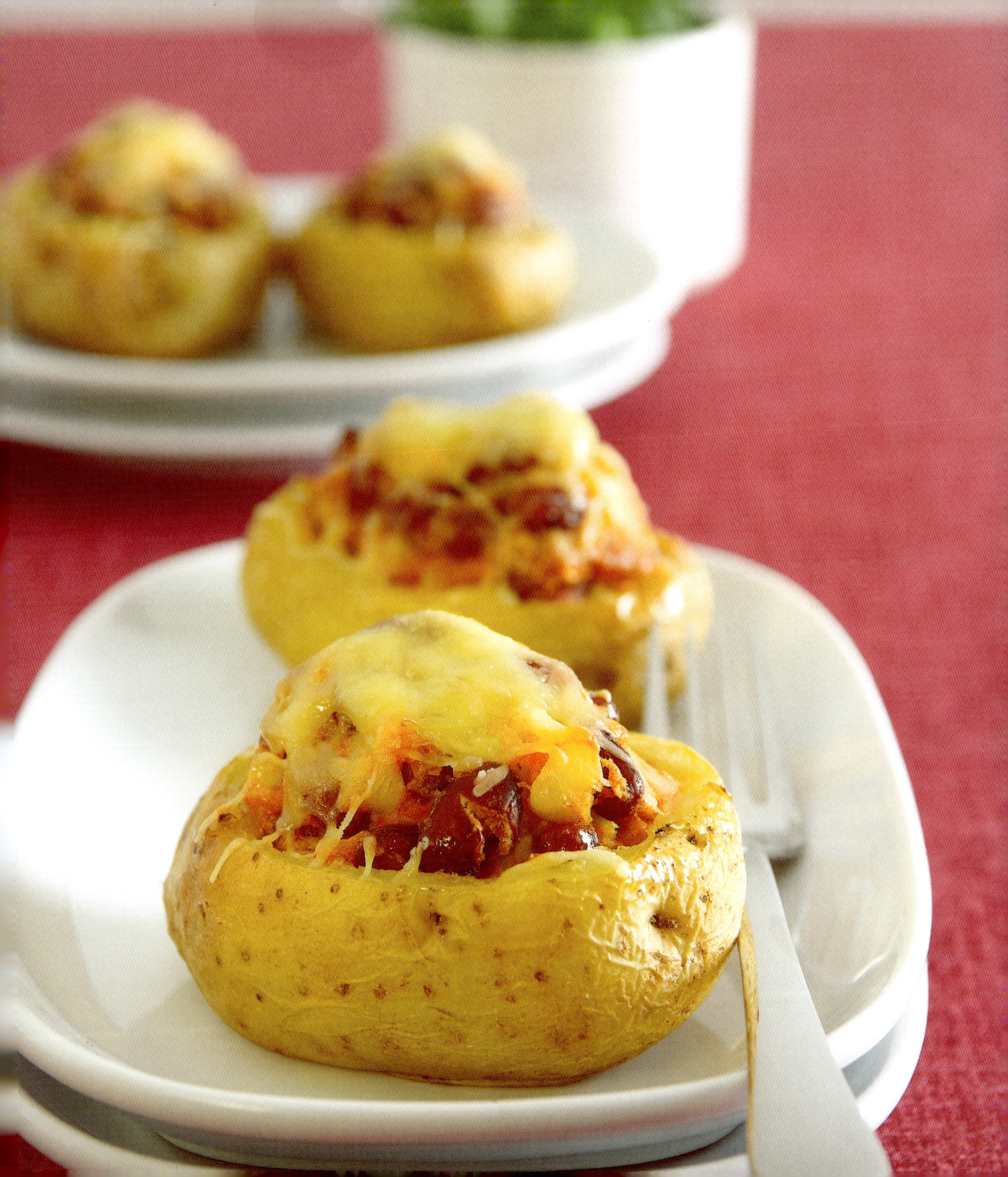

Stuffed baked potatoes

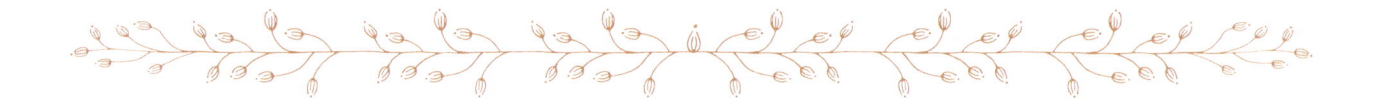

4 large potatoes, scrubbed
1 tablespoon olive oil
1 teaspoon rosemary, chopped
1 teaspoon crushed garlic
1 small onion, diced
100 g/3½ oz Gruyere cheese, grated
30 g/1 oz butter
salt and freshly ground black pepper
sour cream, to serve
paprika, to garnish

serves 4

Preheat the oven to 220°C/425°F/Gas mark 7.

Shave a little from one side of each potato so that each stands upright in a baking dish. Rub the exterior with olive oil and salt. Bake for 45 minutes to 1 hour. Remove from the oven and using oven gloves slice a lid off each potato.

Scoop out the flesh into a bowl and break up. Combine with the salt, pepper, rosemary, garlic, onion, butter and 40 g/1½ oz of the cheese. Fill the potatoes skins with this mixture.

Return the potatoes to the baking dish. Sprinkle with remaining grated cheese, and pop the lids back on. Return to the oven until softened and cooked through, about 20 minutes. Serve with a dollop of sour cream and a dusting of paprika.

Entrées

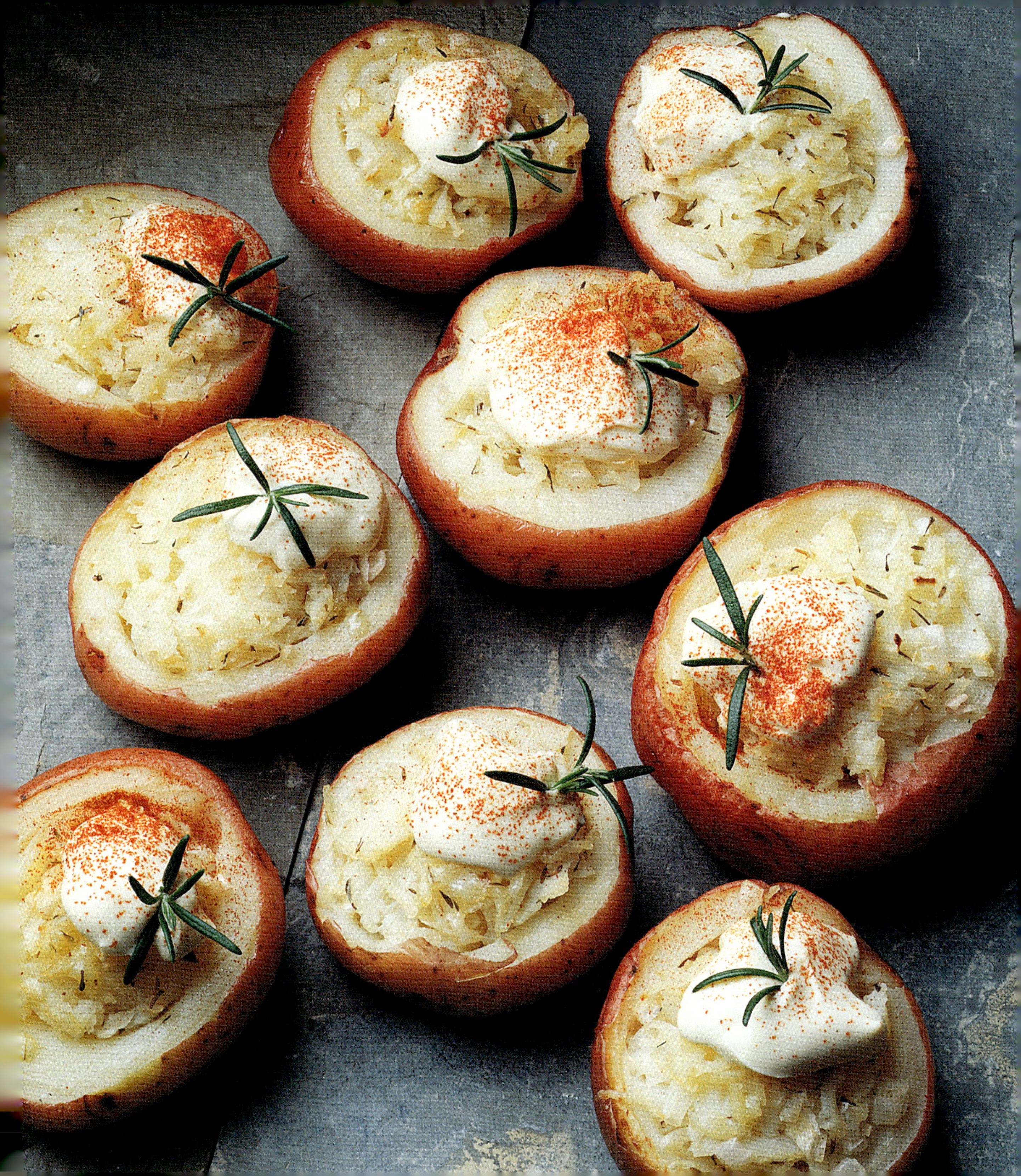

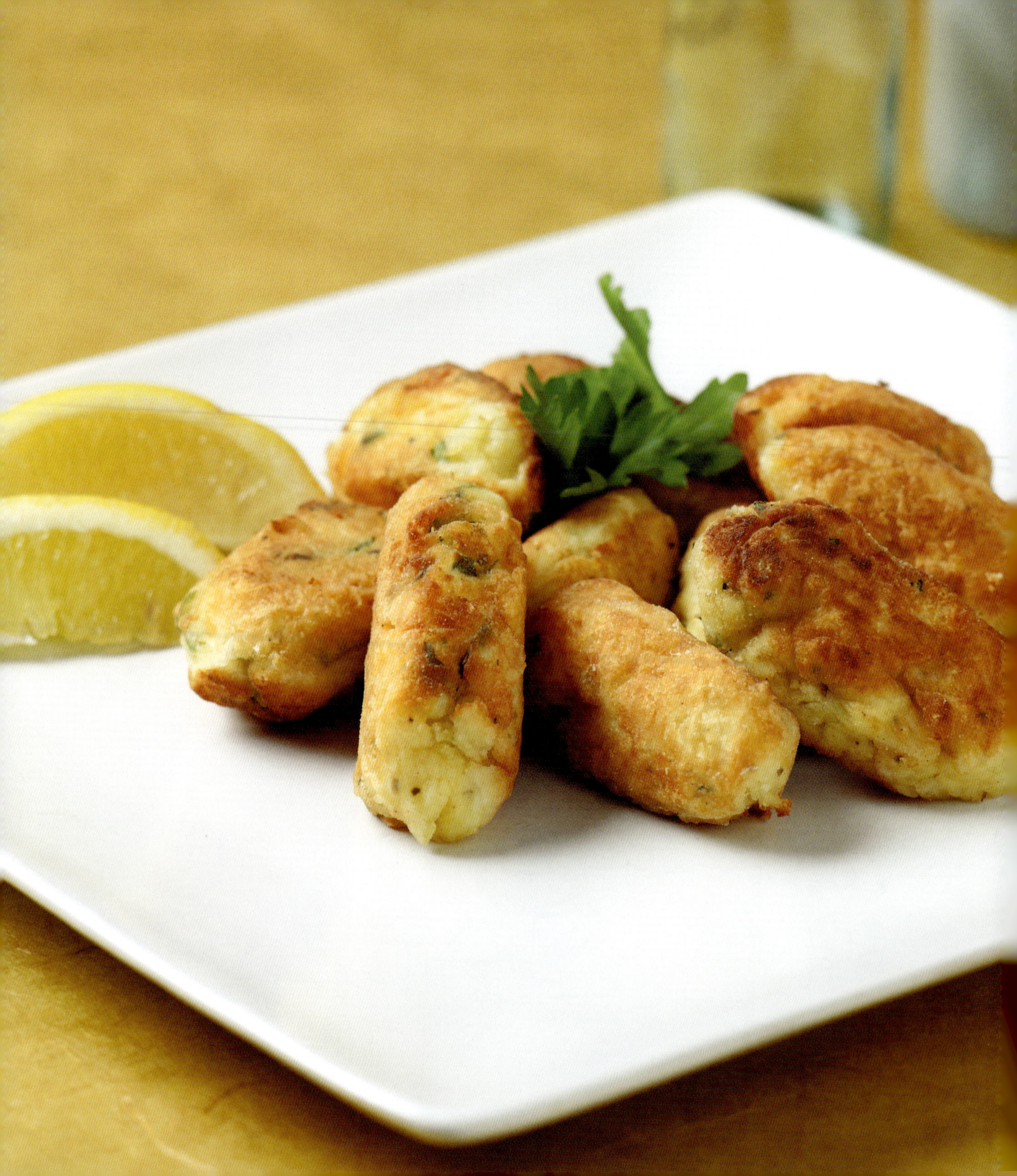

Potato croquettes

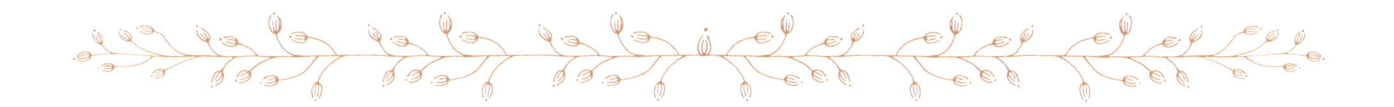

450 g/1 lb potatoes, peeled
30 g/1 oz butter
1 egg yolk
2 tablespoons hot milk
seasoned flour
2 eggs, beaten
breadcrumbs, for coating
olive oil, for frying
salt and freshly ground black
   pepper, to taste

serves 6

Cook the potatoes in a large pan of boiling, salted water until tender. Drain, then return to the pan to dry through. Mash and then press through a sieve or potato ricer. Return to the pan. Add the butter, egg yolk, milk, and salt and pepper, and beat until smooth. Divide the mixture into small pieces similar to the shape of wine corks.

Roll each croquettes in seasoned flour, then brush with egg and roll in breadcrumbs. Deep-fry in hot oil until golden brown.

Entrées

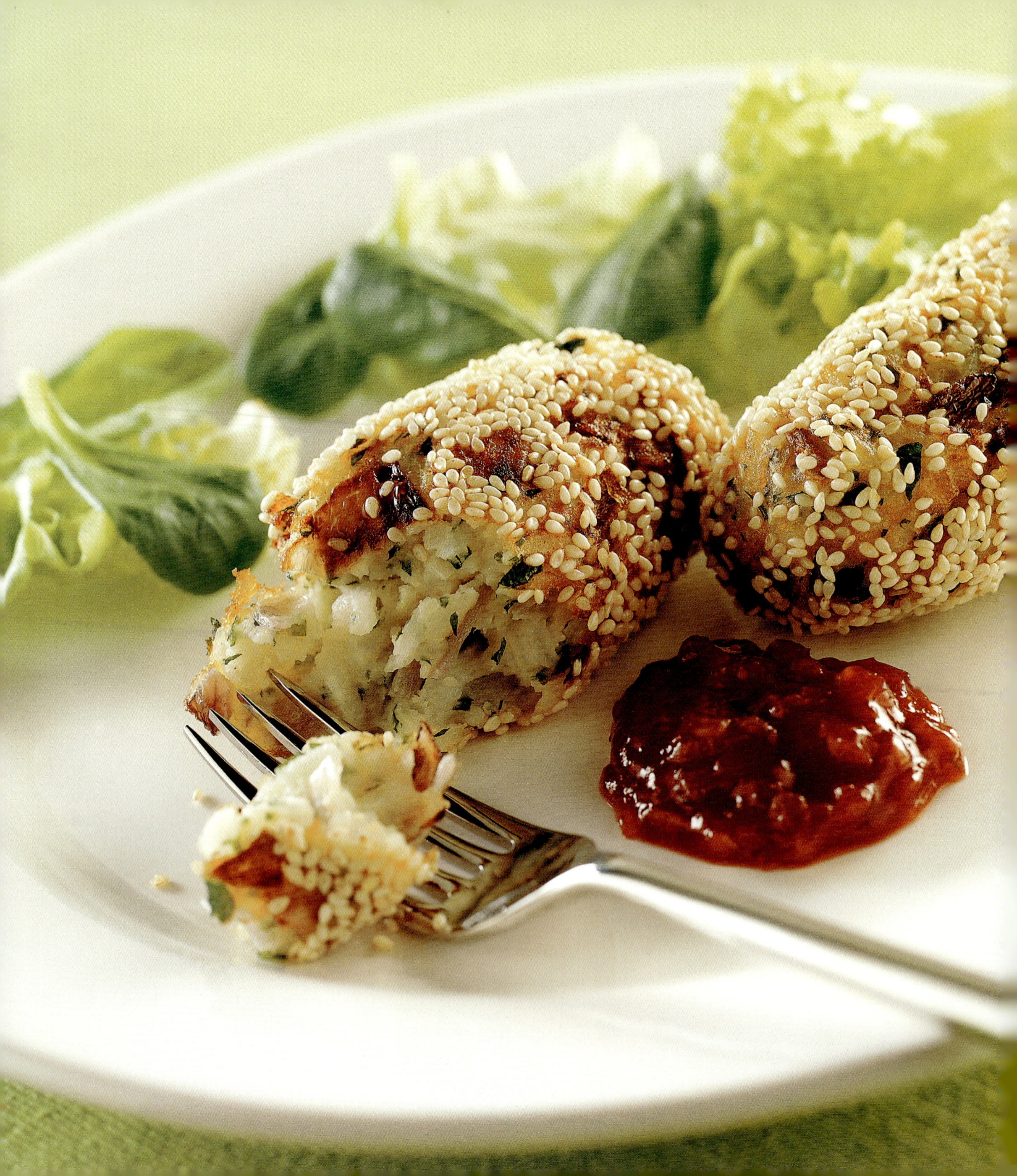

Potato and parsley croquettes

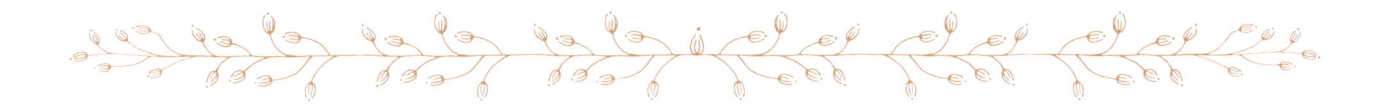

100 g/3½ oz/½ cup long grain rice
2 large potatoes, cut into chunks
2 red onions, finely chopped
1 garlic clove, crushed
⅓ cup/3 tablespoons fresh parsley, chopped
75 g/2½ oz/½ cup sesame seeds
sunflower oil, for frying
salt and freshly ground black pepper

serves 4

Combine the rice with 175 ml/6 fl oz/¾ cup water in a large pan. Bring to the boil, reduce the heat to low, cover and cook for 15 minutes. Remove the pan from heat and spread the rice on a plate. Leave for 1 hour, or until cooled completely, fluffing it up with a fork occasionally.

Meanwhile, put the potatoes into a large saucepan of boiling salted water and simmer for 15–20 minutes, until tender. Drain, mash and combine with the cooled rice, seasoning, onions, garlic and parsley. Mix thoroughly.

Shape the mixture into 8 croquettes with your hands, then roll in the sesame seeds. Heat 1 cm/⅜ in of oil in a large, heavy frying pan and fry the croquettes for 2–3 minutes, turning constantly until crisp and browned all over.

Entrées

French onion flans

250 g/9 oz prepared puff pastry
oil, for greasing
170 g/6 oz mature Cheddar
   (tasty) cheese, grated

FOR THE ONION FILLING
60 g/2 oz butter
6 onions, sliced
3 eggs
400 ml/14fl oz/1¾ cups sour
   cream or natural (plain) yogurt
1 teaspoon ground nutmeg
1½ teaspoon horseradish relish

Preheat the oven to 200°C/400°F/Gas mark 6. Roll out the pastry and use to line six lightly greased 10 cm/4 in flan tins.

To make the filling, melt the butter in a frying pan and cook the onions over a low heat for 10–15 minutes, or until golden. Divide into six portions and spread over the base of the flans.

Place eggs, sour cream or yogurt, nutmeg and horseradish in a bowl and mix to combine. Pour the egg mixture into the flan cases and sprinkle with grated cheese. Bake for 20 minutes, or until the flans are set.

serves 6

Entrées

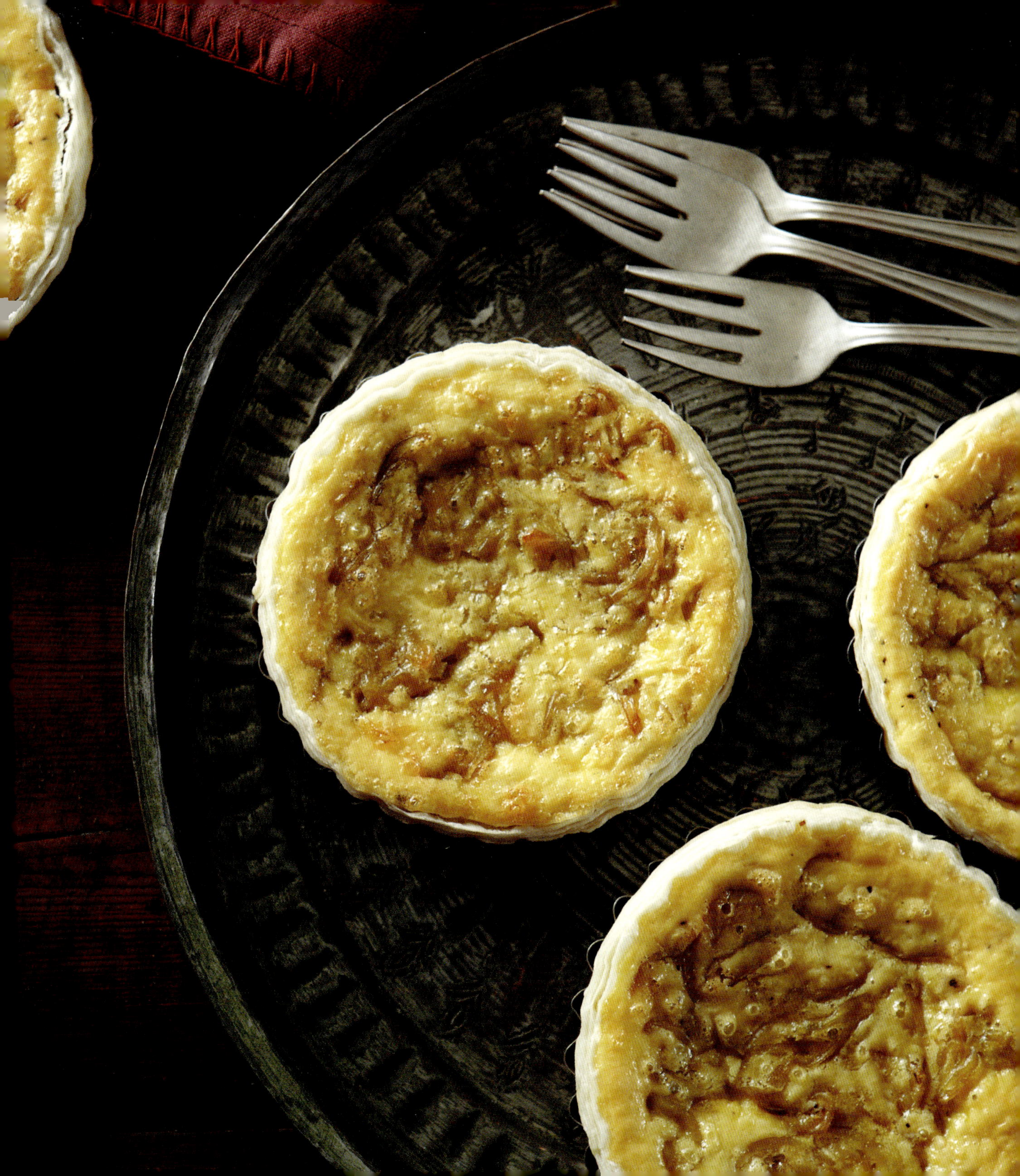

Mains

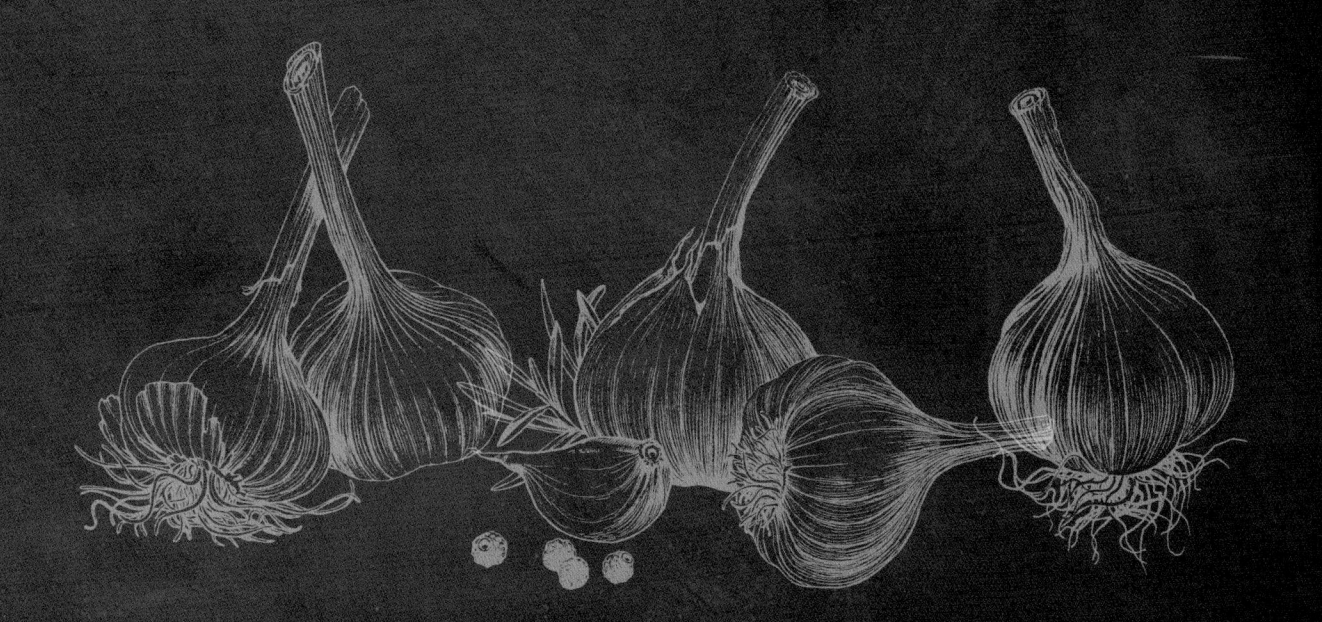

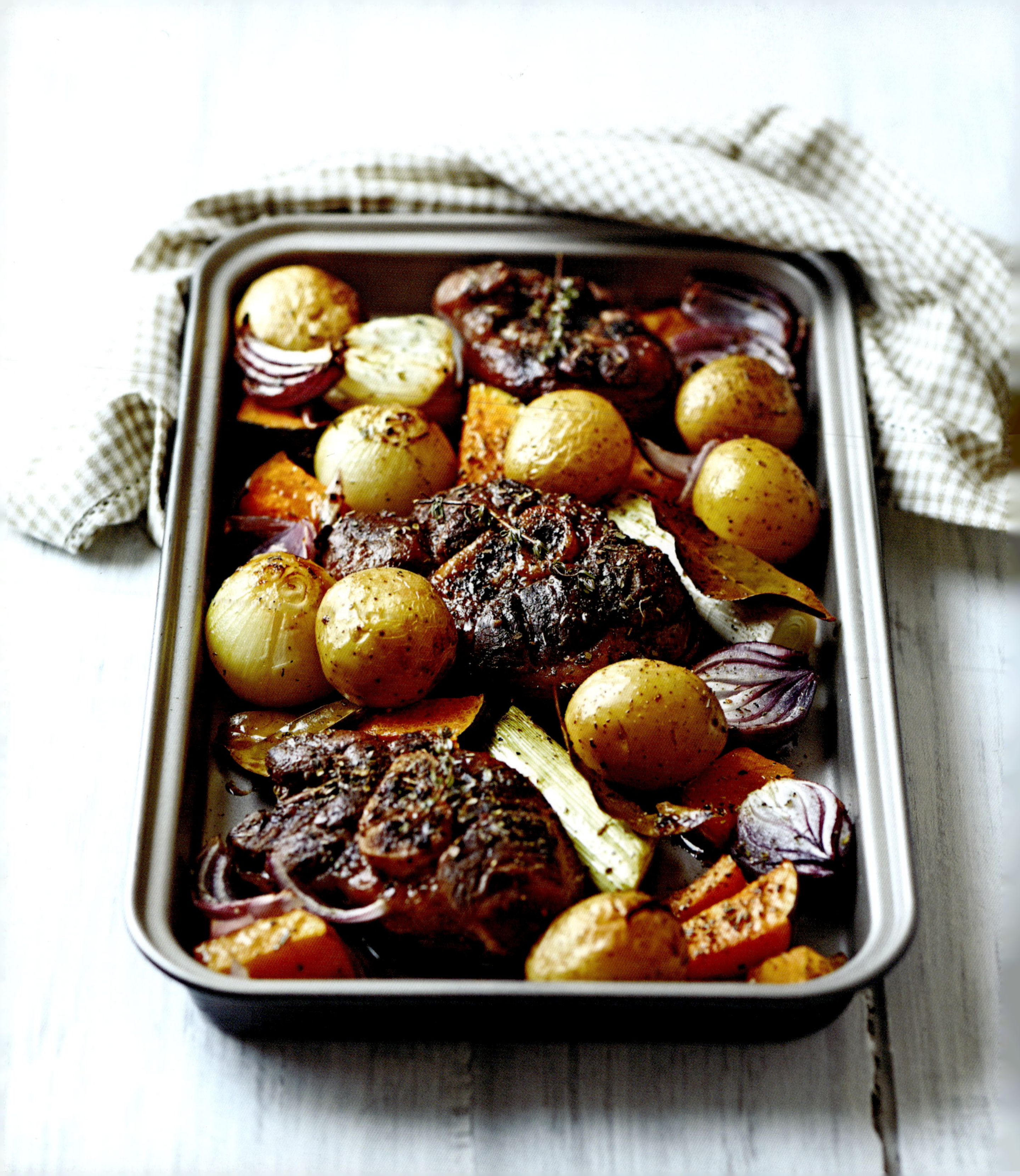

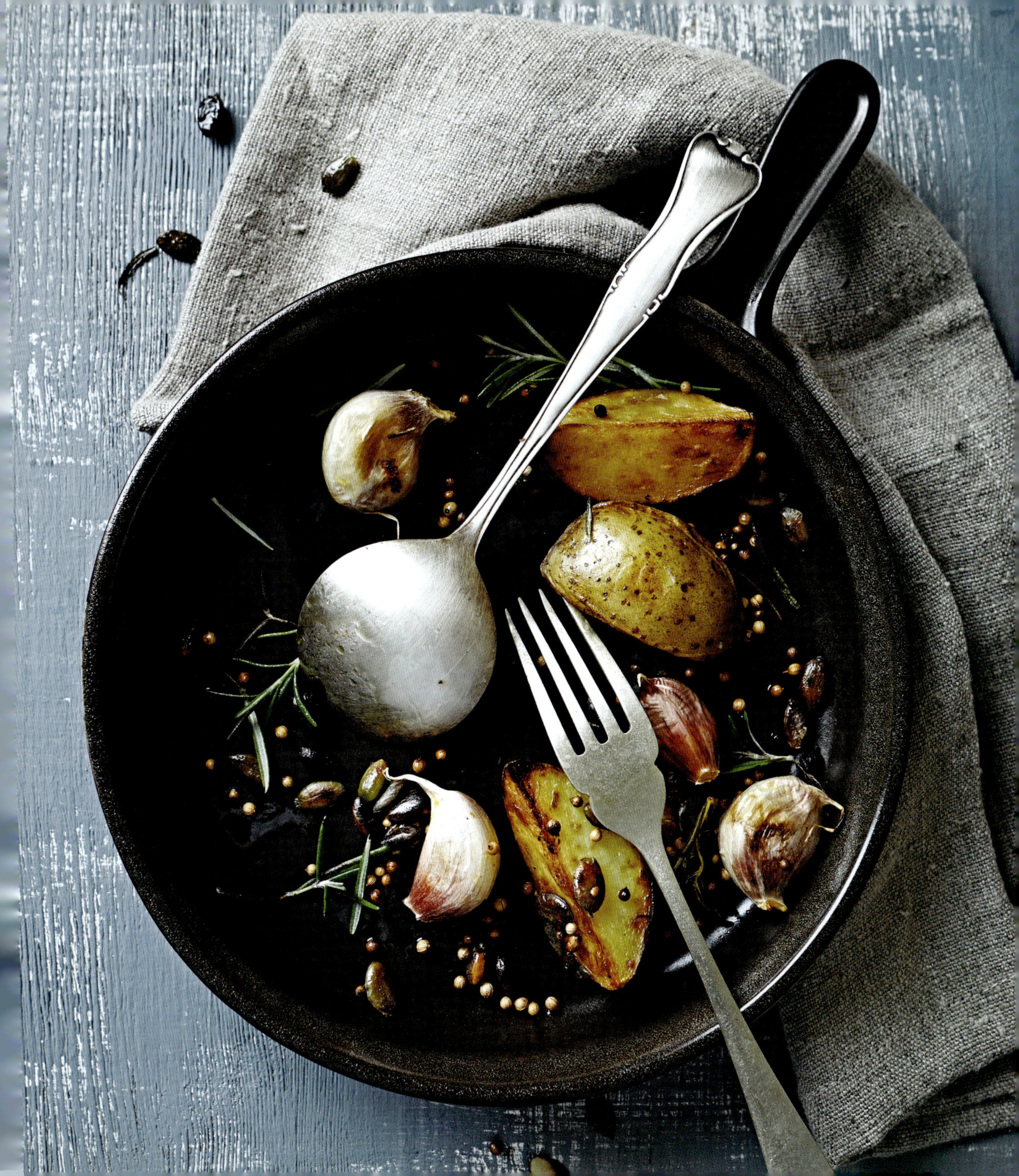

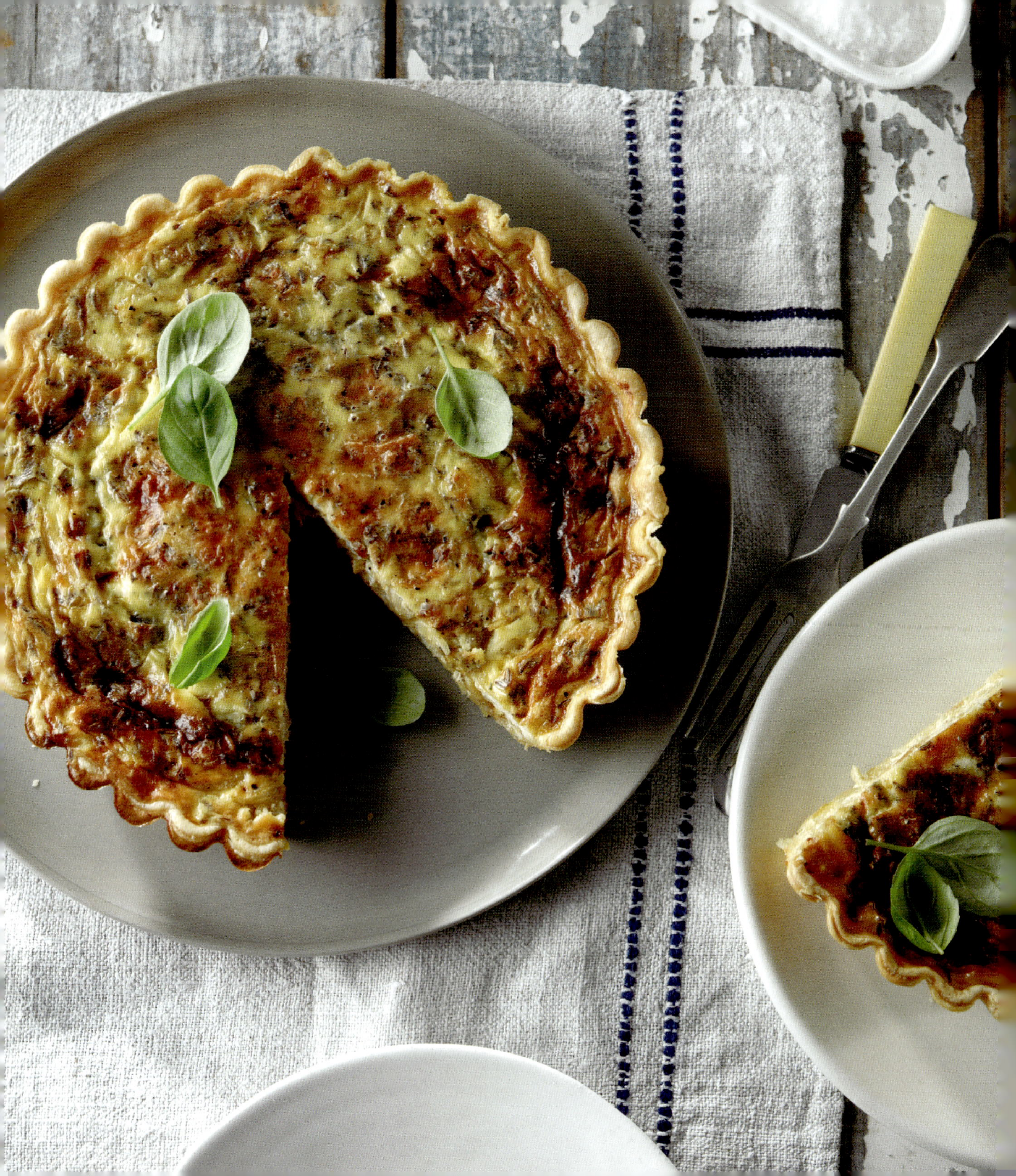

Blue cheese and onion quiche

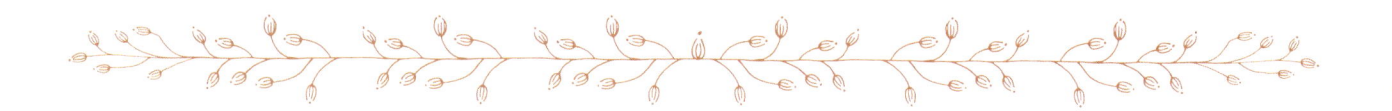

370 g/13 oz prepared shortcrust pastry
2 tablespoons butter
3 onions, thinly sliced
2 garlic cloves, crushed
3 eggs
60 g/2 oz blue cheese, crumbled
250 ml/8 fl oz/1 cup milk
175 ml/6 fl oz/¾ cup sour cream
freshly ground black pepper
2 teaspoons caraway seeds

serves 4

Roll out the pastry to fit a 23 cm/9 in fluted flan tin. Place a sheet of baking paper over the pastry, and half-fill with rice. Bake in a moderately hot oven for 8 minutes. Remove the rice and paper, then bake for another 10 minutes, or until golden brown.

Meanwhile, melt the butter in a frying pan, and add the onion and garlic and stir-fry over low heat for about 10 minutes, or until the onions are soft and golden brown. Spoon evenly over the pastry.

Preheat the oven to 160ºC/325ºF/Gas mark 3.

In a bowl, lightly beat the eggs, then add the cheese, milk, sour cream, pepper and caraway seeds and gently pour over the onions.

Bake for 30 minutes, or until just set and lightly browned.

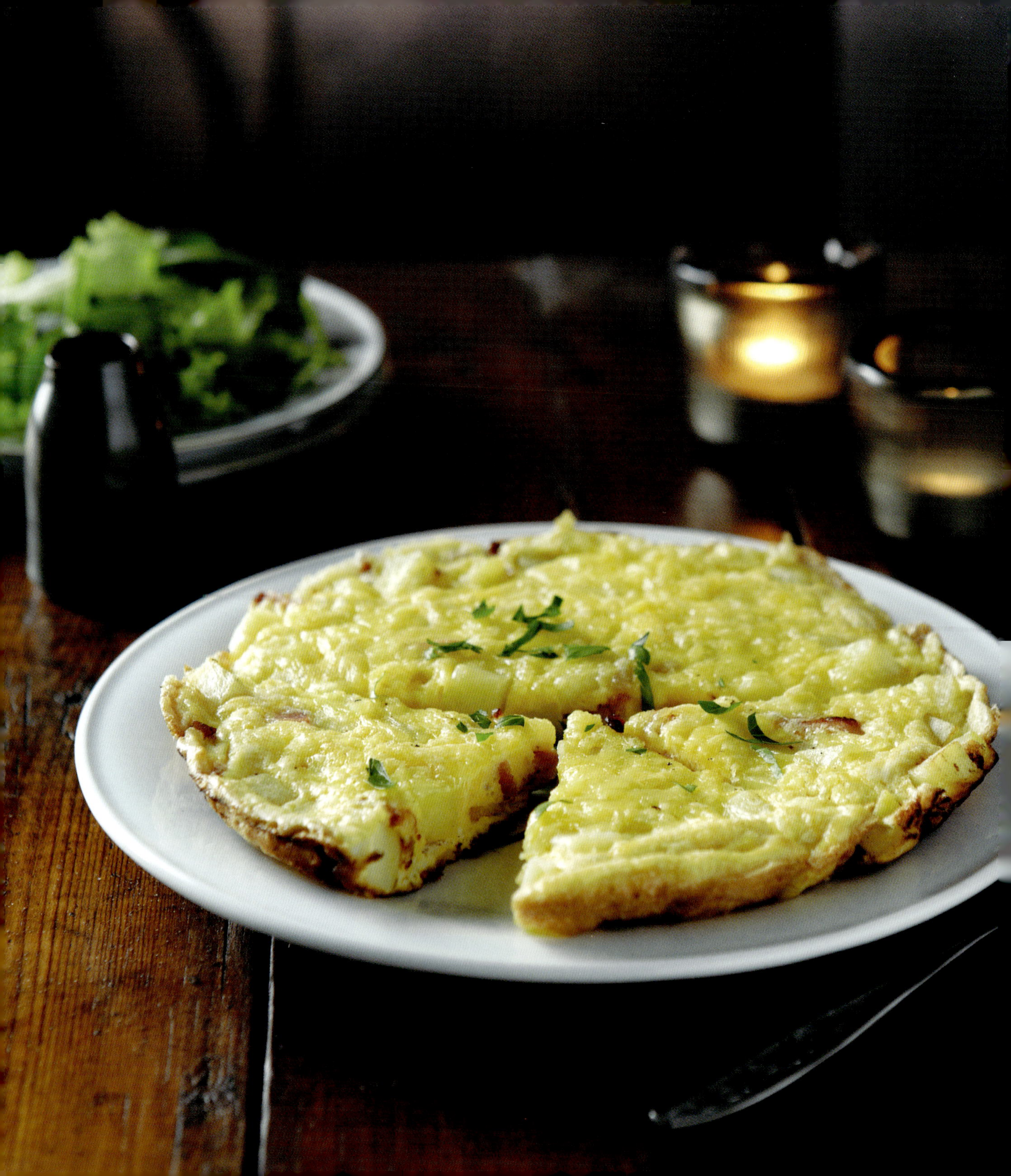

Cheesy potato frittata

1 potato, cooked and cooled
2 rashers (strips) bacon
4 eggs
freshly ground black pepper
2 tablespoons butter
30 g/1 oz mature Cheddar (tasty) cheese, grated

serves 4

Cut the potato into 12 mm/½ in cubes. Set aside. Trim the rind from the bacon, then cut the bacon into strips. Set aside. Break the eggs into a bowl. Add black pepper to taste. Whisk, then set aside.

Melt the butter in a frying pan set over medium heat. Add the bacon and fry, stirring, for 2–3 minutes, or until cooked. Add the potato to the pan. Cook, stirring, for 5 minutes, or until the potato is brown. Pour the egg mixture into the pan. Reduce the heat to low. Fry for 10 minutes, or until the frittata is almost set.

Preheat the grill (broiler) to high. Sprinkle the top of the frittata with cheese. Place the pan under the grill. Cook for 2–3 minutes, or until the cheese melts. Cut into wedges to serve.

Mains

Potato and pea omelette

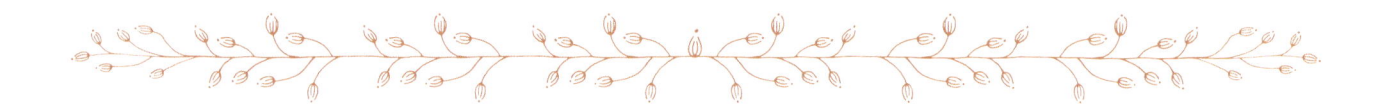

1 teaspoon vegetable oil or butter
1 small slice ham, chopped
1 small potato, finely chopped
1–2 tablespoons peas or sweet corn kernels
1 egg, lightly beaten
2 tablespoons milk

Heat the oil or butter in a small frying pan over a medium heat. Add the ham, potato and peas or sweet corn and cook, stirring frequently for 5–10 minutes, or until the potato is tender.

Place the egg and milk in a bowl and whisk to combine. Pour the egg mixture over the potato mixture in the pan, reduce the heat and cook without stirring for 3–4 minutes, or until the omelette is just firm.

serves 1

Mains

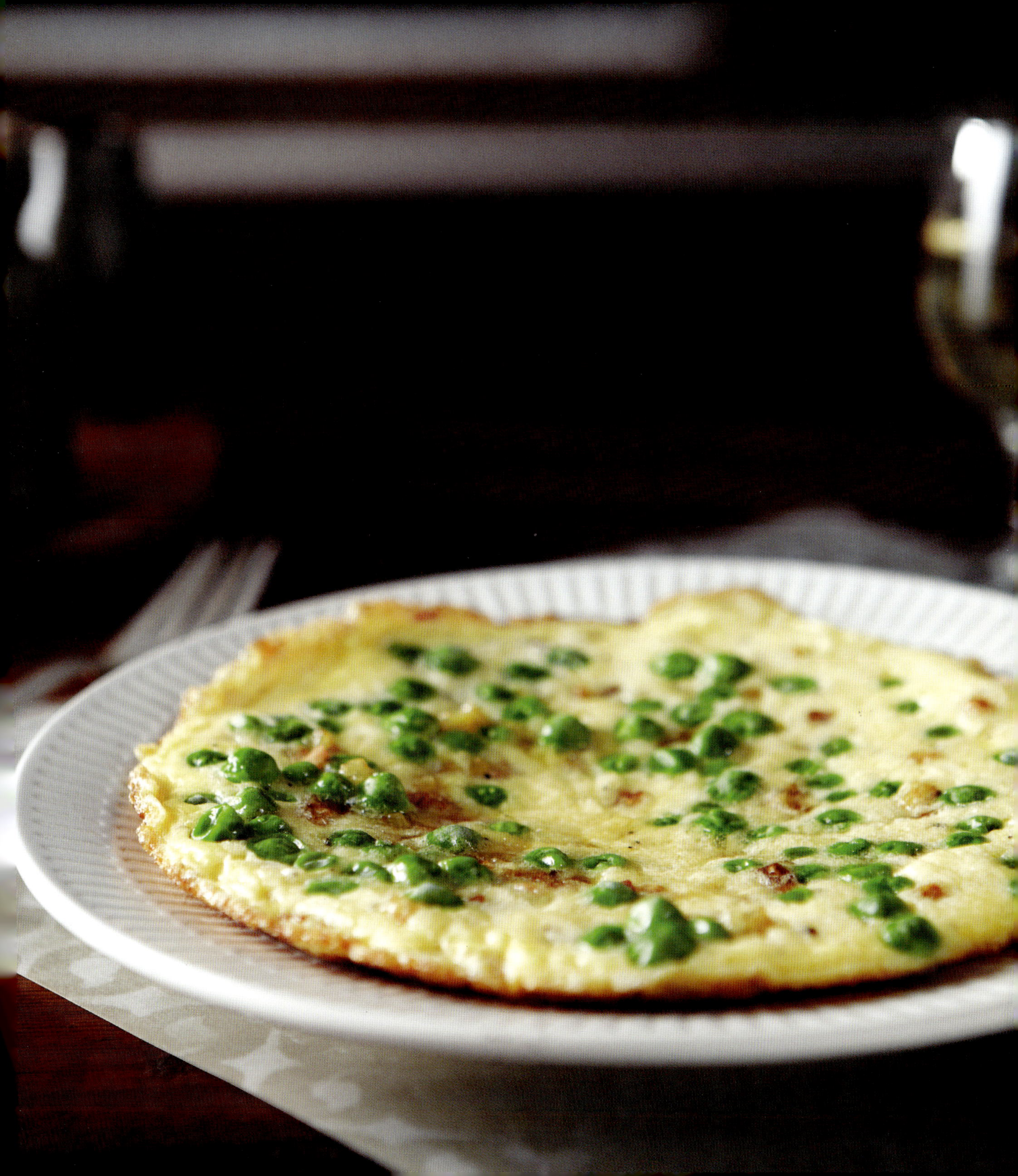

Roasted vegetable and broccoli couscous

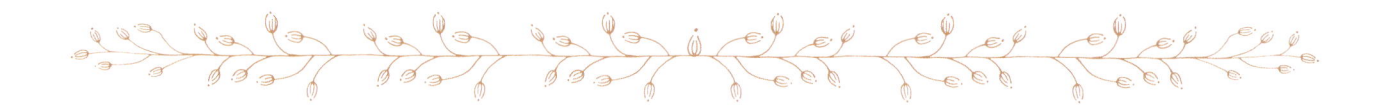

4 parsnips, cut into chunks
2 sweet potatoes, cut into small chunks
1 large turnip, chopped into small chunks
2 cloves garlic, crushed
5 tablespoons olive oil
4 tablespoons apple or redcurrant jelly
300 g/10½ oz couscous
500 g/1 lb 2 oz tomatoes, chopped
handful each of fresh parsley, chives and basil, chopped
juice of 1 lemon
300 g/10½ oz broccoli, cut into florets
salt

serves 4

Preheat the oven to 200°C/400°F/Gas mark 6.

Cook the parsnips in a large pan of boiling salted water for 2 minutes, then drain. Place in a roasting tin with the sweet potatoes, turnip, garlic and 3 tablespoons of oil, turning to coat. Sprinkle with salt, then bake for 30 minutes, or until lightly browned.

Melt the apple or redcurrant jelly in a pan with 4 tablespoons of water for 2–3 minutes, until it turns syrupy. Turn the vegetables in the tin and drizzle with the syrup. Return to the oven for 10 minutes or until browned and glossy.

Meanwhile, prepare the couscous according to the packet instructions.

Heat the rest of the oil in a frying pan and cook the tomatoes for 2–3 minutes, until softened. Add the couscous and heat through, then mix in the herbs and lemon juice.

Meanwhile, steam the broccoli florets over a pan of boiling water for 6 minutes, or until tender, then drain. Serve the couscous with the roasted vegetables and broccoli arranged on top.

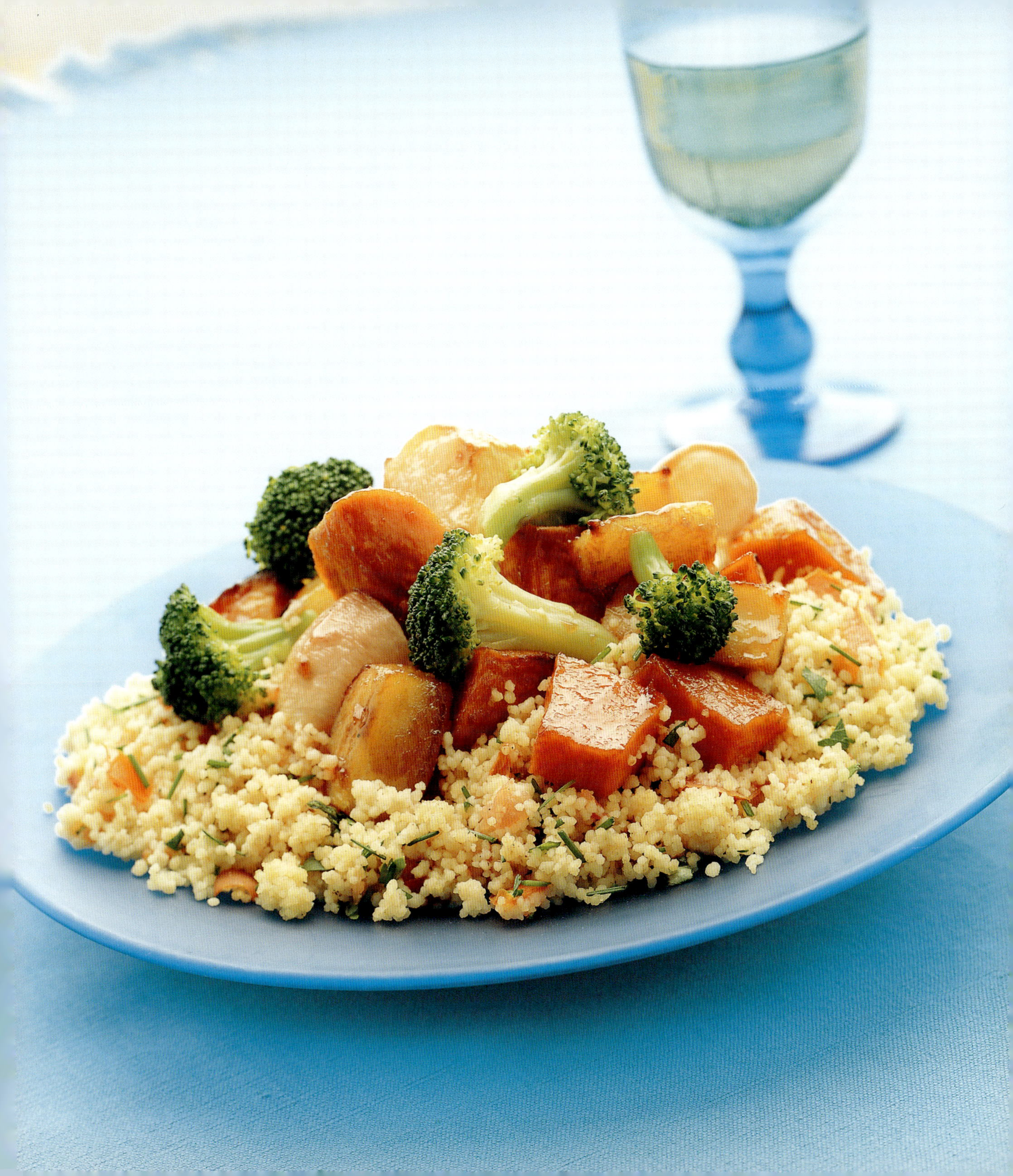

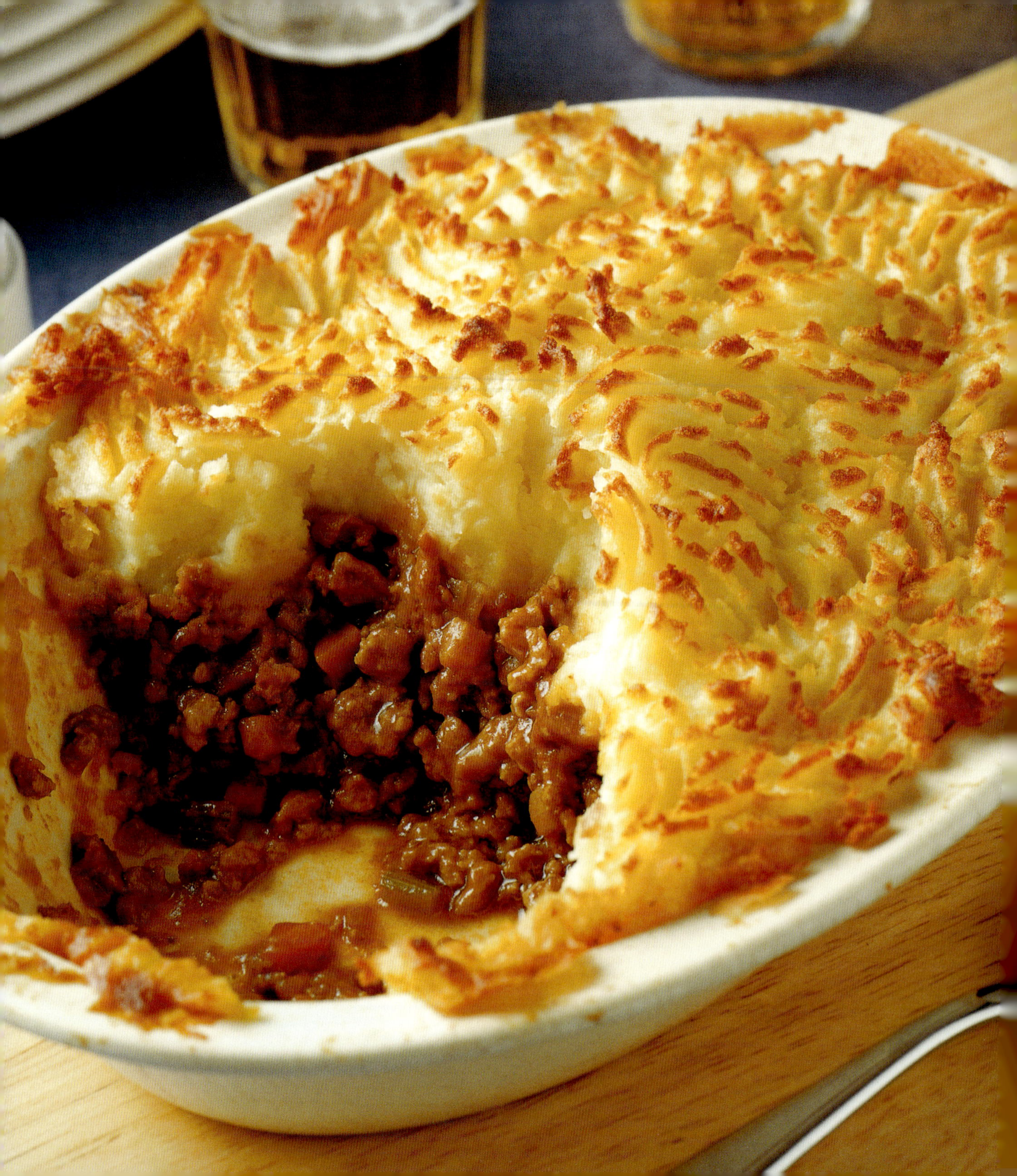

Shepherd's pie

1 tablespoon olive oil
1 onion, finely chopped
2 tomatoes, skinned and chopped
350 g/12 oz minced (ground) beef, cooked
½ teaspoon mixed herbs
salt and pepper, to taste
300 ml/½ pint beef stock
500 g/1 lb 2 oz mashed potato
30 g/1 oz butter

serves 4

Preheat the oven to 190°C/375°F/Gas mark 5.

In a frying pan, heat the olive oil and fry the onion for 3 minutes. Add the tomatoes and meat and heat together for 2–3 minutes. Stir in the herbs, seasoning and stock—add less stock if you desire a thicker consistency.

Put the meat mixture into a pie dish and cover with mashed potato. Use a fork to score the top. Dot tiny pieces of butter around on the potato to help it brown.

Bake in the centre of the oven until the top is crisp and brown, 30–35 minutes.

Mains

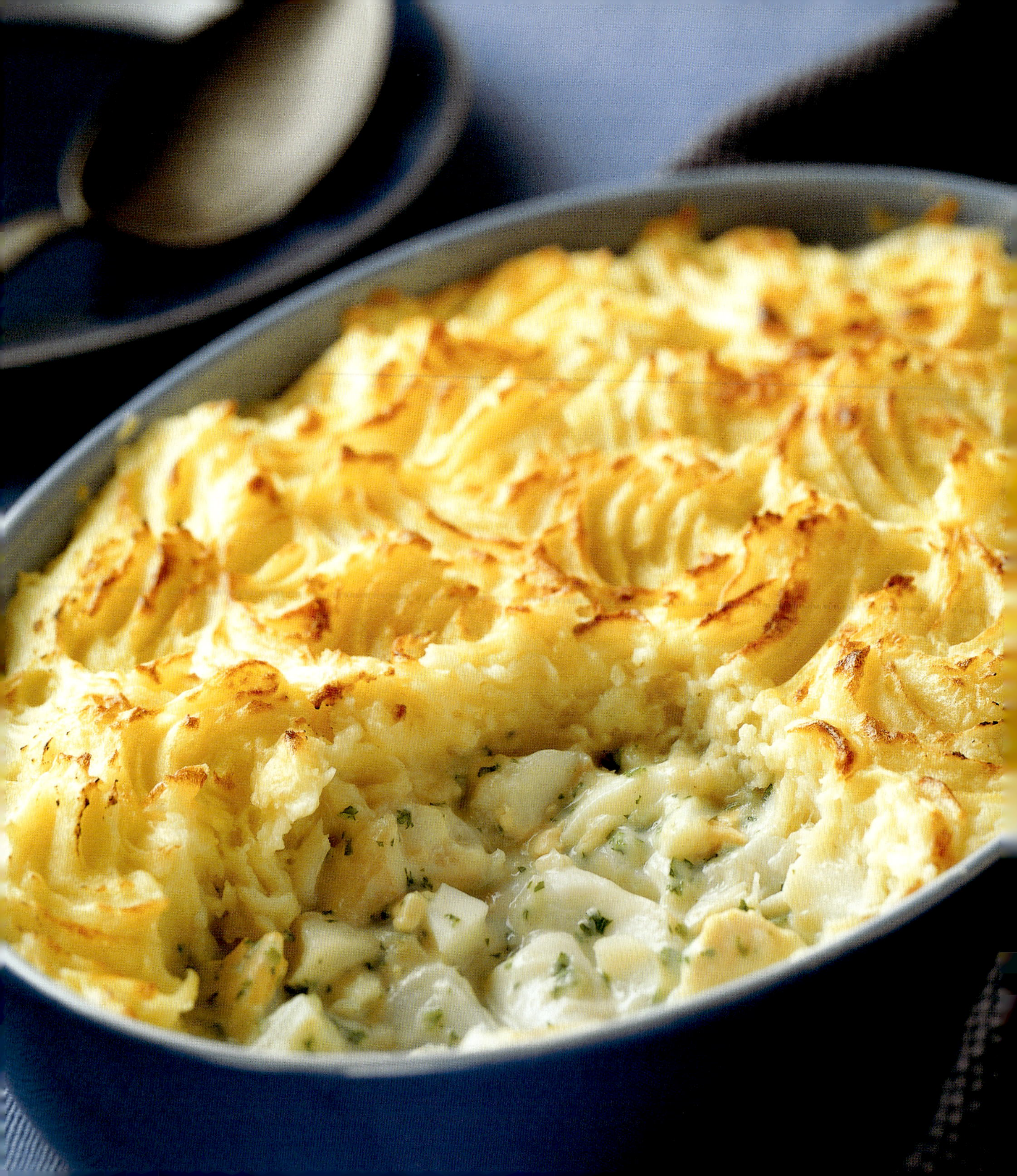

Fish pie

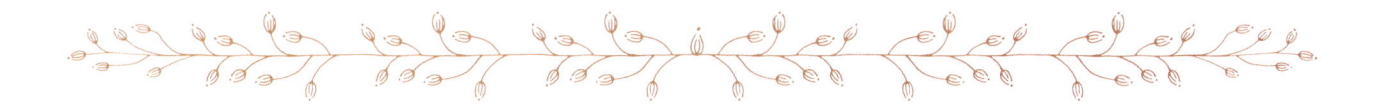

500 g/1 lb 2 oz potatoes, peeled and cut into even-sized pieces
75 g/2½ oz butter
500 g/1 lb 2 oz cod fillets
250 g/9oz smoked haddock fillets
2 eggs, beaten
375 ml/12 fl oz/1½ cups whole milk
45 g/1½ oz plain (all-purpose) flour
⅓ cup/3 tablespoons fresh parsley, finely chopped
salt and freshly ground black pepper

serves 4

Cook the potatoes in a pan of salted boiling water for 20 minutes, or until tender. Drain and return to the pan. Mash well, then mix in two-thirds of the butter.

Meanwhile, boil the eggs, for 10 minutes, in a small pan. Cool under cold running water, then shell and roughly chop.

Preheat the oven to 200°C/400°F/Gas mark 6.

Place the cod and haddock fillets skin-side down in a frying pan that is large enough to hold them in a single layer. Cover with milk and cook over a medium heat for 10 minutes, or until the fish turns opaque. Drain, reserving the milk for the sauce, then remove and discard any skin and bones. Flake the fish into an ovenproof dish. Add the eggs and parsley.

To make the sauce, put the remaining butter in a large pan. Melt over a low heat, add the flour and stir to form a smooth paste. Cook for 2 minutes, stirring, to remove the raw flavour of the flour. Add the milk little by little, stirring constantly so there are no lumps. Cook for 5–7 minutes, until thickened. Season well, then pour over the fish. Smooth the mashed potato on top. Bake for 30 minutes, or until the top turns golden.

Mains

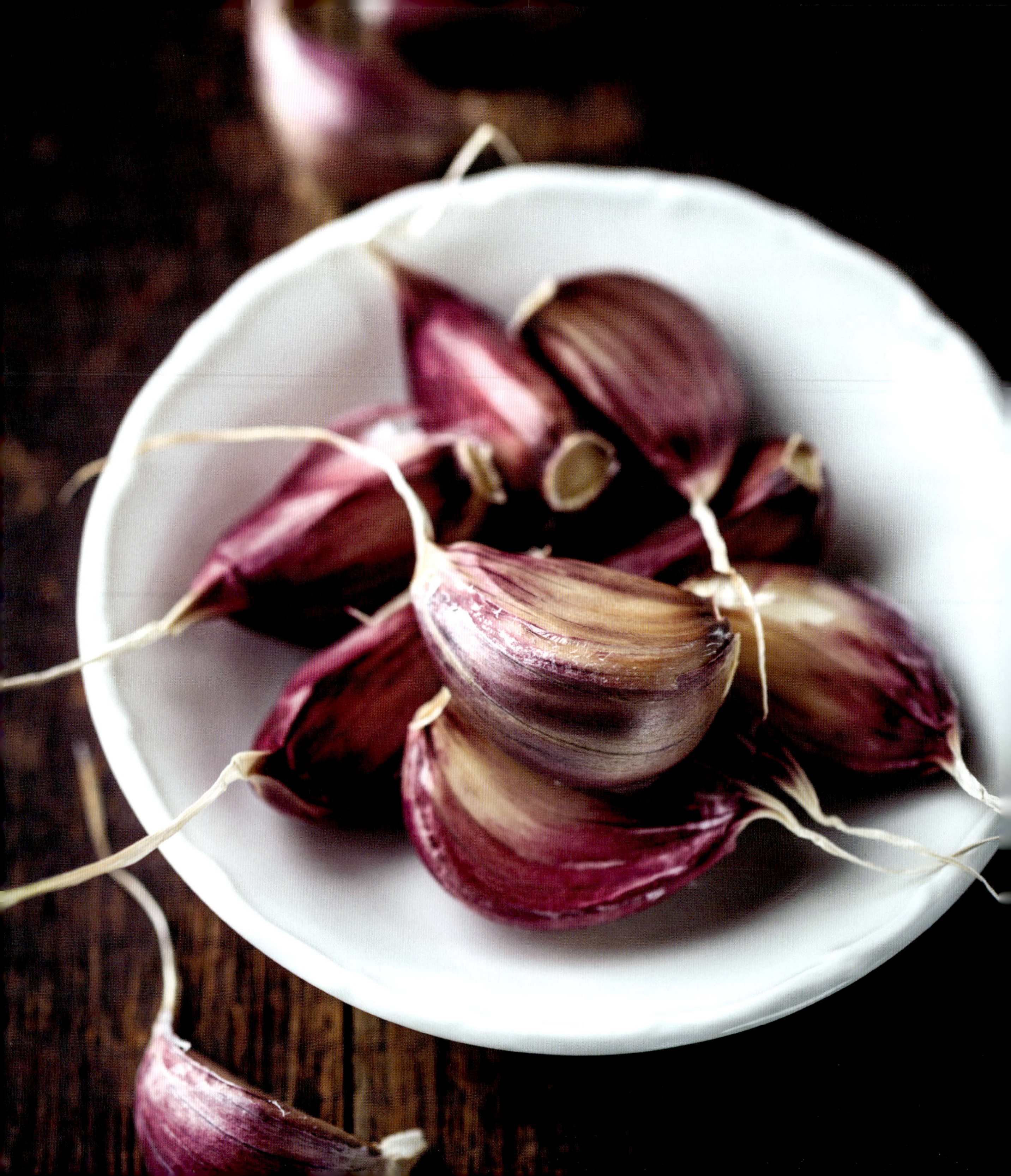

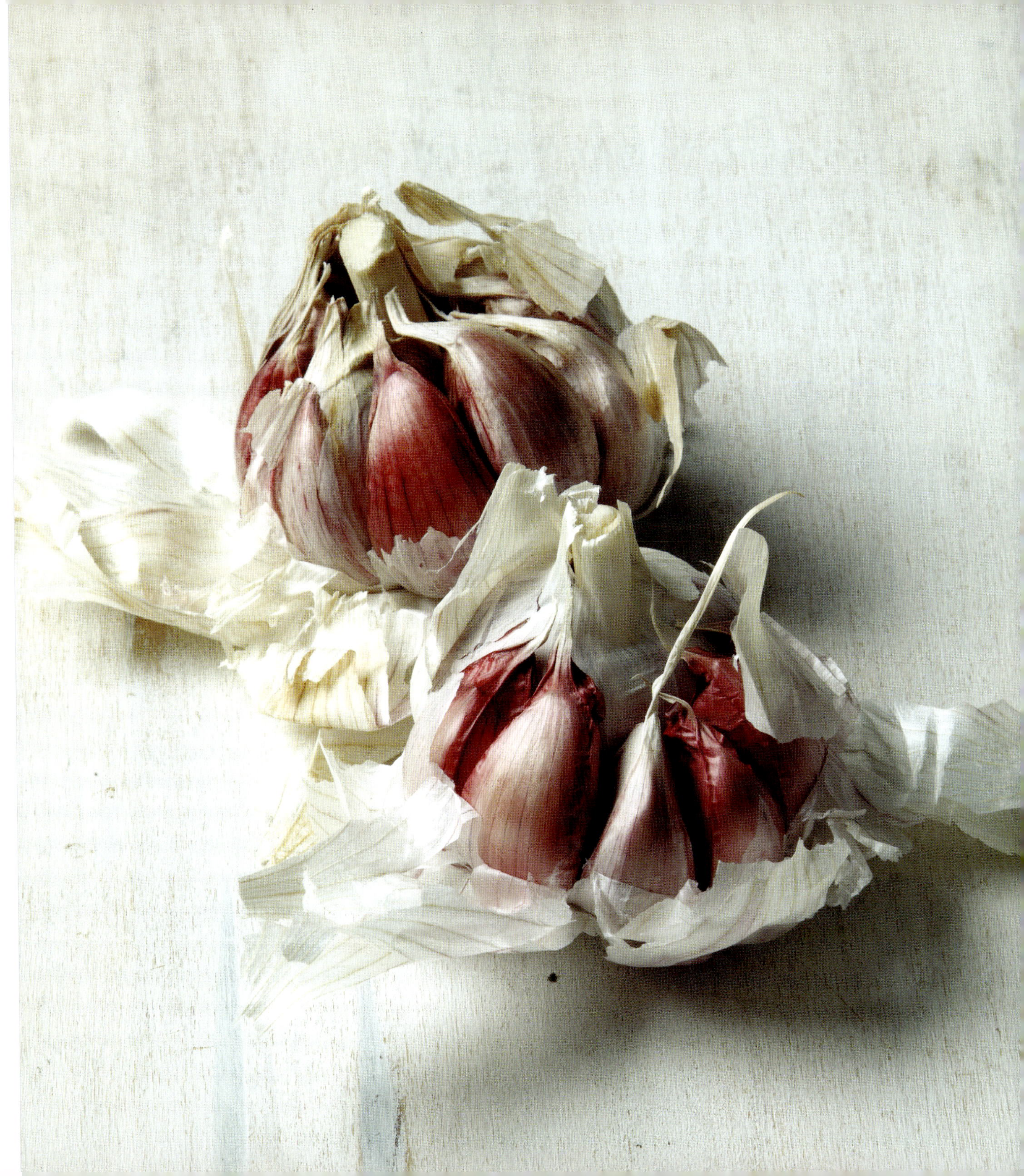

Vegetable and lentil curry

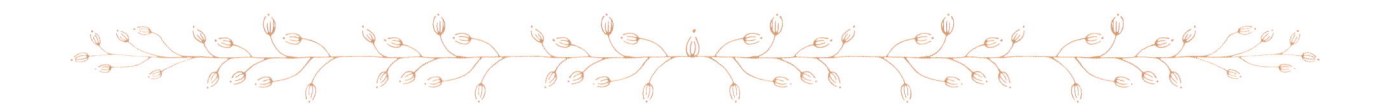

1 tbsp olive oil
1 onion, sliced
1 clove garlic, crushed
1 tsp ground cumin
1 tsp ground coriander
1 tsp ground turmeric
2 carrots, sliced
3½ oz/100 g red lentils
7 oz/200 g can tomatoes, mashed with the juice
1½ cups/12 fl oz/ 350 ml vegetable stock or water
1 tsp chilli sauce
1 lb/450 g pumpkin or potatoes, cut into 1 in/2.5 cm cubes
½ cauliflower, cut into florets
2 tbsp blanched almonds
freshly ground black pepper
4 tbsp natural yogurt

Heat oil in a large pan, add onion, garlic, cumin, coriander, turmeric and carrots and cook for 5 minutes or until onion is soft.

Stir in lentils, tomatoes and stock or water and bring to the boil. Reduce heat, cover and simmer for 15 minutes.

Add chilli sauce, pumpkin or potatoes and cauliflower and cook for 15-20 minutes longer or until pumpkin or potatoes are tender. Stir in almonds and black pepper to taste. To serve, ladle curry into bowls and top with a spoonful of yogurt.

serves 4

Mains

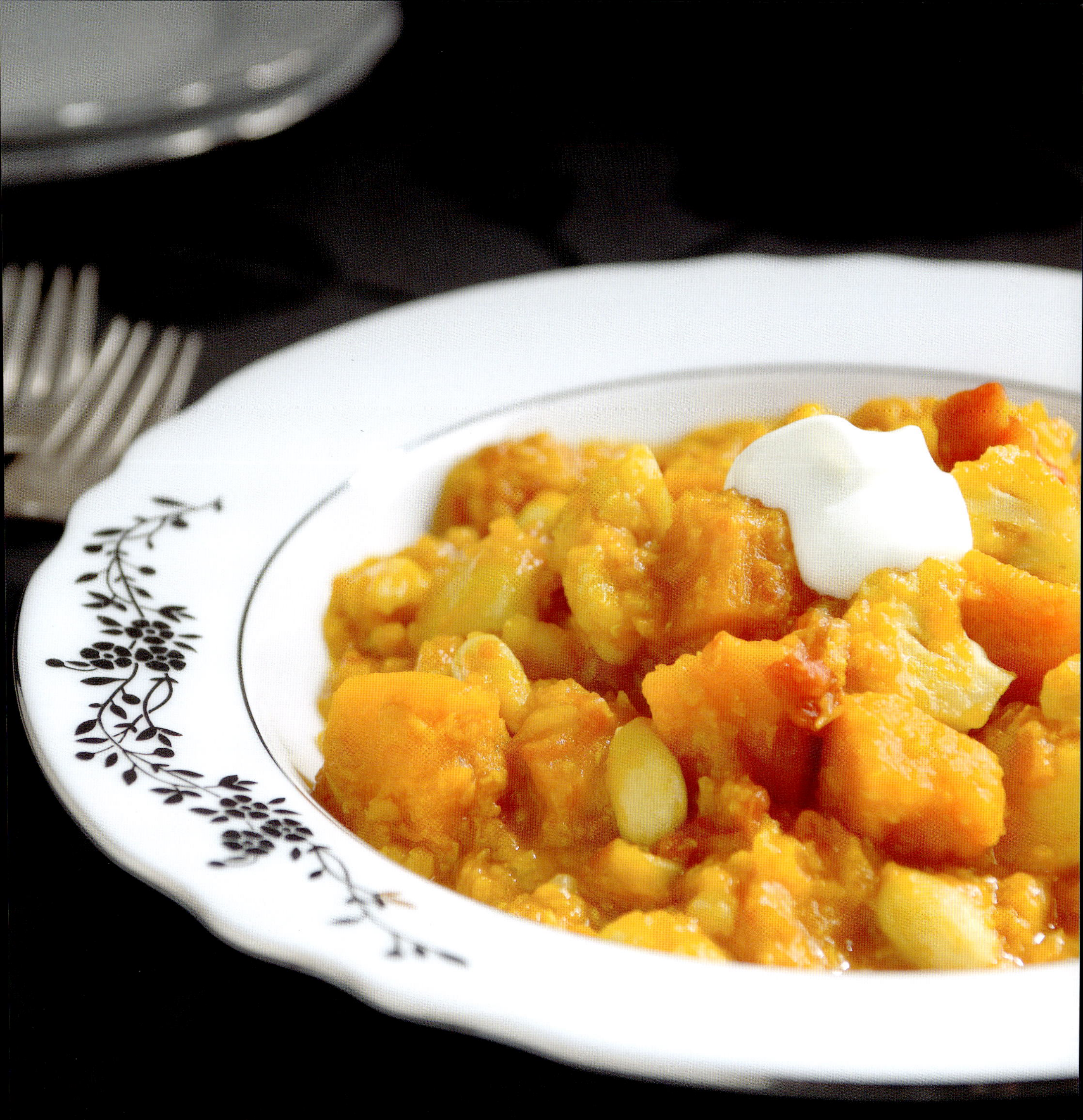

Grilled pork chops with baked sweet potato

2 pork chops (2.5 cm/1 in thick)
4 tablespoons Worcestershire sauce
2 teaspoons crushed garlic

FOR THE BAKED SWEET POTATO
2 sweet potatoes
salt and freshly ground black pepper
lemon pepper
brown sugar
cinnamon
butter

serves 2

Put the chops in a non metallic bowl and marinate with the Worcestershire sauce and garlic for 2 hours.

One hour later, preheat the oven to 180°C/350°F/Gas mark 4 When the oven reaches temperature bake the sweet potato for at least 1 hour.

Grill (broil) the chops on both sides until cooked through so there is no pink in the middle, about 20 minutes total.

Cut the sweet potato with a sharp knife before serving. Top with butter and salt and pepper; butter and lemon pepper; or butter with brown sugar and cinnamon.

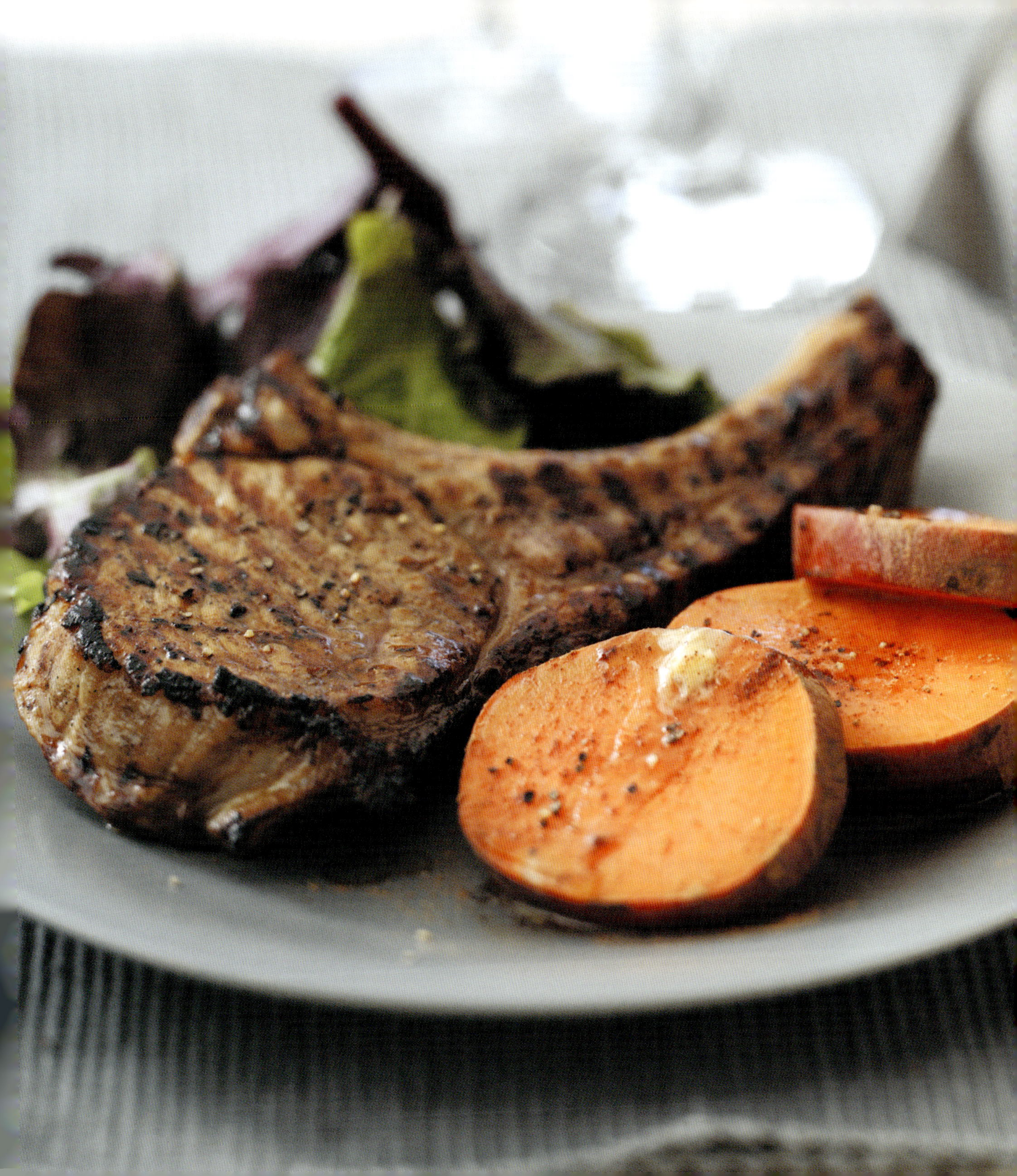

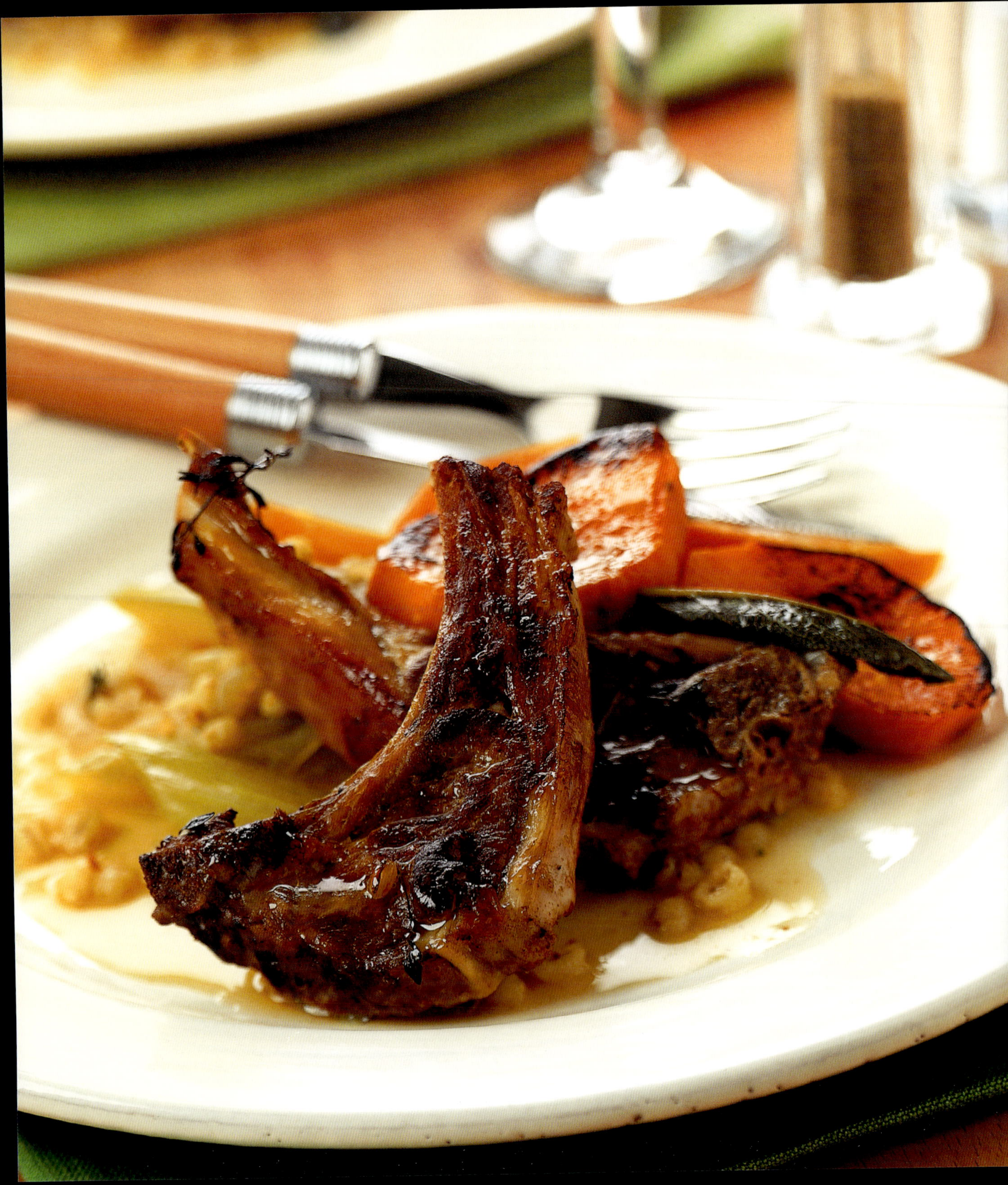

Lamb and sweet potato stew

8 lamb cutlets
1 tablespoon olive oil
500 ml/17 fl oz/2 cups chicken stock
2 onions, thinly sliced
500 g (1 lb 2 oz) sweet potatoes, cut into 1 cm/$^3/_8$ in-thick slices
200 g (7 oz) carrots, chopped
4 celery sticks, chopped
6 fresh sage leaves
4 fresh thyme sprigs
salt and black pepper
3 tablespoons pearl barley

serves 4

Preheat the oven to 180°C/350°F/Gas mark 4. Trim any excess fat from the cutlets. Heat the oil in a large, heavy frying pan and fry the cutlets for 1–2 minutes on each side until brown (you may have to do this in batches). Remove the cutlets and set aside. Discard the oil and add a little stock to the pan. Bring to the boil, stirring and scraping the base of the pan to remove the sediment, then tip into the casserole with the rest of the stock.

Place half the onions in a large ovenproof casserole dish. Top with one-third of the sweet potatoes, then add half the carrots and celery, and all the sage, thyme and cutlets. Season, then sprinkle over the barley. Repeat the layering and top with the remaining sweet potatoes. Pour over the stock and cover.

Cook for 1½ hours or until the lamb is tender, checking occasionally and adding more stock or water if the casserole is becoming too dry. Remove the lid and increase the heat to 230°C/450°F/Gas mark 8. Cook for 8–10 minutes, until the potatoes have browned.

Mains

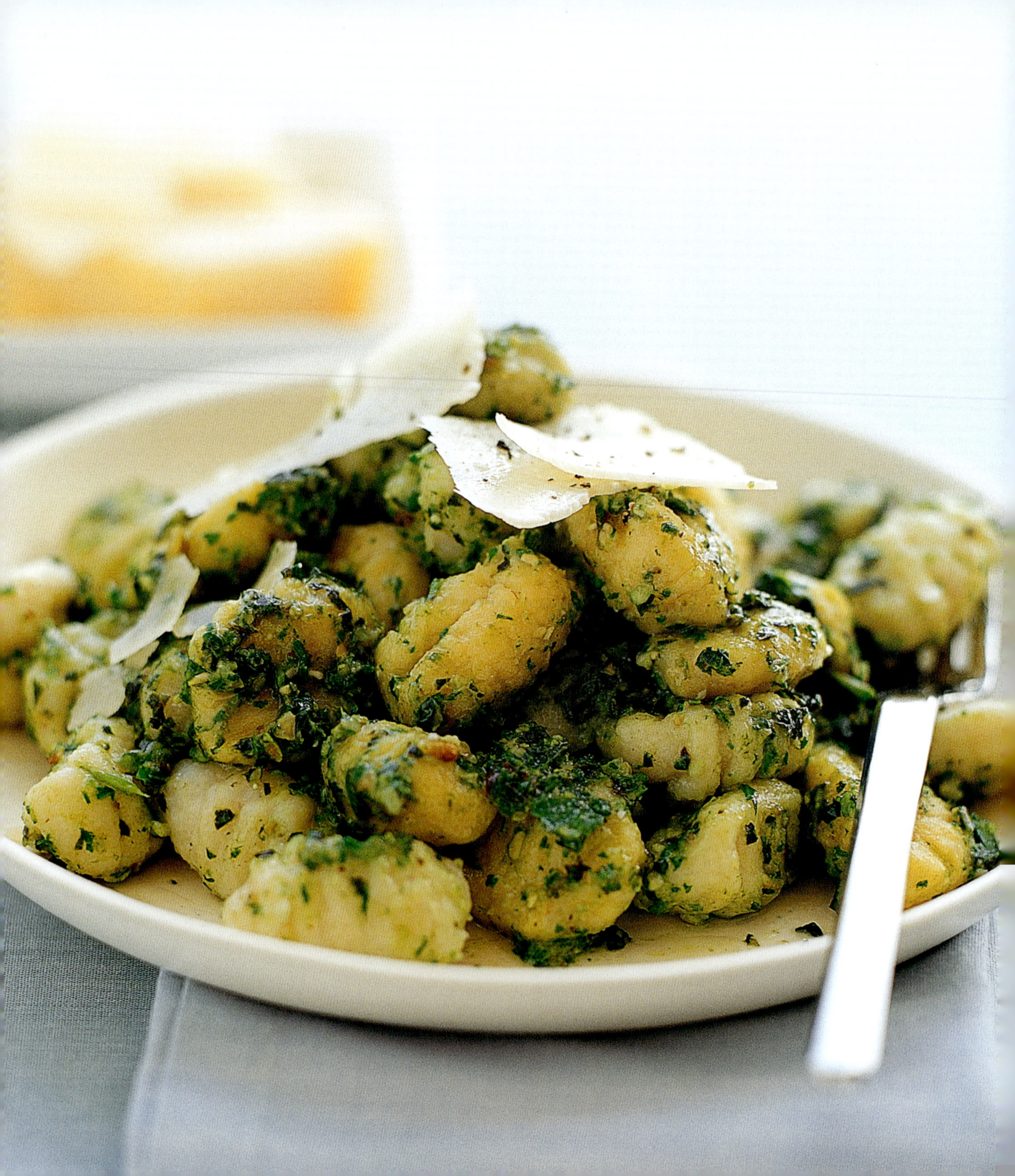

Gnocchi with spinach, arugula and basil pesto

500 g/1 lb 2 oz fresh potato gnocchi
2 cups baby spinach leaves, washed
2 cups baby arugula (rocket) leaves, washed
1 cup fresh basil leaves
2 garlic cloves
4 tablespoons pine nuts, toasted
30 g/1 oz/¼ cup Parmesan, grated, plus extra to serve
2 tablespoons extra virgin olive oil
freshly ground black pepper

Cook the gnocchi in a large pan of rapidly boiling water, just until they float to the surface. Remove with a slotted spoon, drain well and set aside. Keep warm.

Steam the spinach until it wilts, drain and squeeze out any excess moisture.

Put the spinach, arugula, basil, garlic, pine nuts and Parmesan in a food processor and process until smooth. With the motor running, gradually add the oil and process to form a smooth paste.

Spoon the pesto over the cooked gnocchi and toss to coat. Season with the pepper. Serve garnished with shaved Parmesan.

serves 4

French onion stew

1.5 kg/3 lb 5 oz lean stewing steak, trimmed, and cut into large cubes
2 tablespoons tapioca
400 ml/14 fl oz/1¾ cups beef stock
100 g/3½ oz mushrooms, sliced
60 g (2 oz) butter
6 medium onions, thinly sliced
pinch of salt
60 ml/2 fl oz/¼ cup double (heavy) cream
fresh thyme leaves, to garnish
rice, to serve
thyme, to serve

Combine the beef, tapioca, stock and mushrooms in a slow cooker, cover and cook on high for 4 hours.

Meanwhile, melt the butter in a large heavy frying pan set over low heat. Add the onion and cook, stirring, for 45 minutes or until caramelised and dark brown in colour. Add the caramelised onions to the slow cooker and stir to combine. Continue to cook all the ingredients together for the remaining time.

Just before serving stir through the cream. Serve the stew on a bed of rice, garnished with fresh thyme.

serves 6

Mains

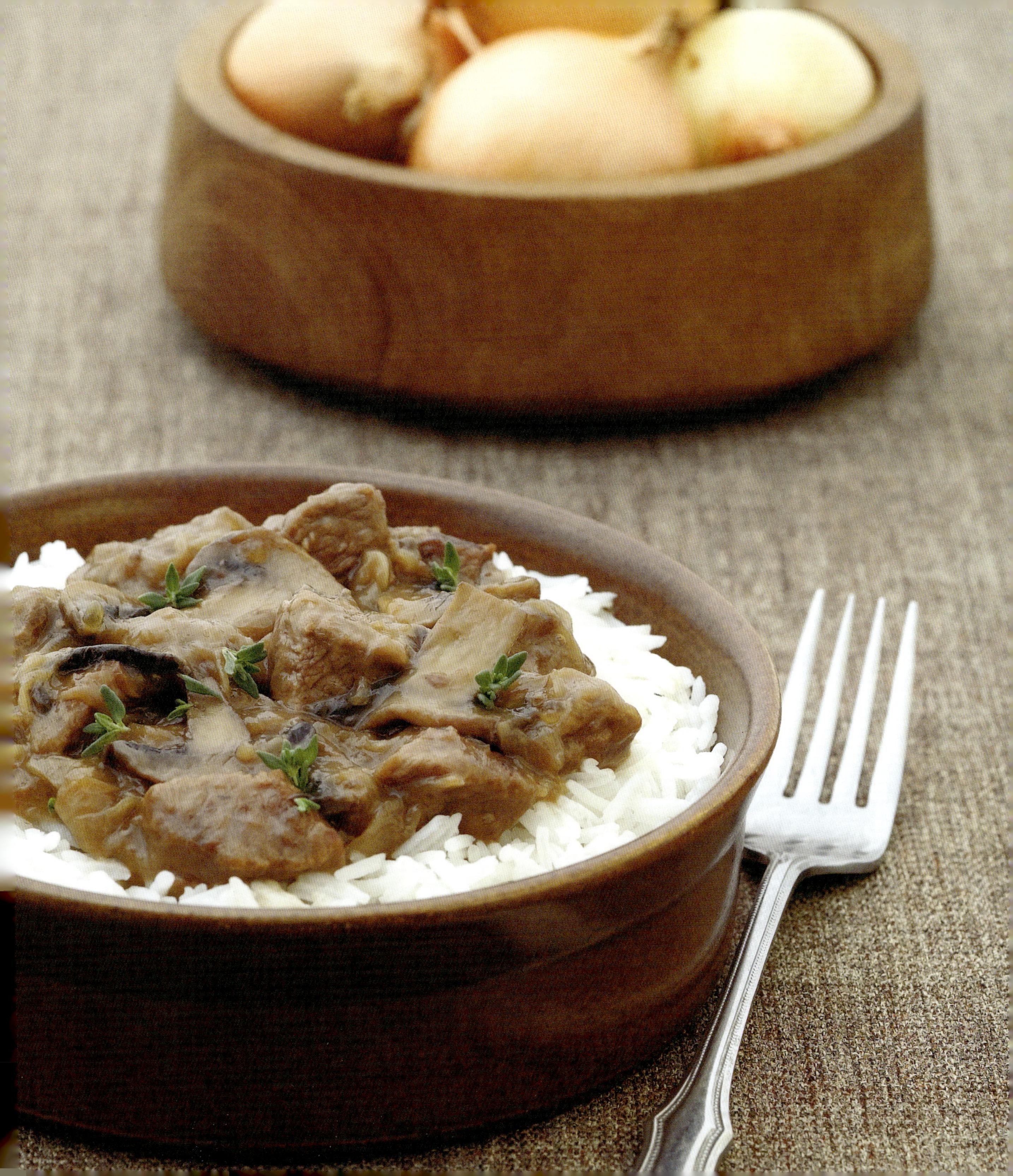

Potato, onion and bacon cake

750 g/1 lb 10 oz potatoes, peeled and coarsely grated
15 g/½ oz butter
2 tablespoons vegetable oil
1 onion, chopped
6 rashers (strips) rindless bacon, cut into 1 cm/³⁄₈ in strips
1 egg, beaten
1 tablespoon all-purpose (plain) flour
2 tablespoons fresh parsley, chopped
freshly ground black pepper

serves 4

Place the grated potatoes in a clean tea towel and squeeze out any excess liquid.

Heat the butter and 1 tablespoon of the oil in a non-stick frying pan. Add the onion and bacon and cook for 5–8 minutes, until the onion has softened and the bacon is cooked through. Clean the pan.

Place the potatoes in a large bowl. Stir in the onion and bacon mixture with the egg, flour, parsley and seasoning. Heat half the remaining oil in the frying pan, add the potato mixture and press into a flat round with a wooden spoon. Cook over a low heat for 10 minutes, or until the base is golden.

Carefully slide the potato cake onto a large plate. Place another large plate over the top and flip the cake so that the uncooked side is underneath. Heat the remaining oil in the pan, then carefully slide the cake back into the pan, uncooked-side down. Cook over a low heat for 10 minutes or until the base is crisp and golden. Serve with a large mixed salad.

Mains

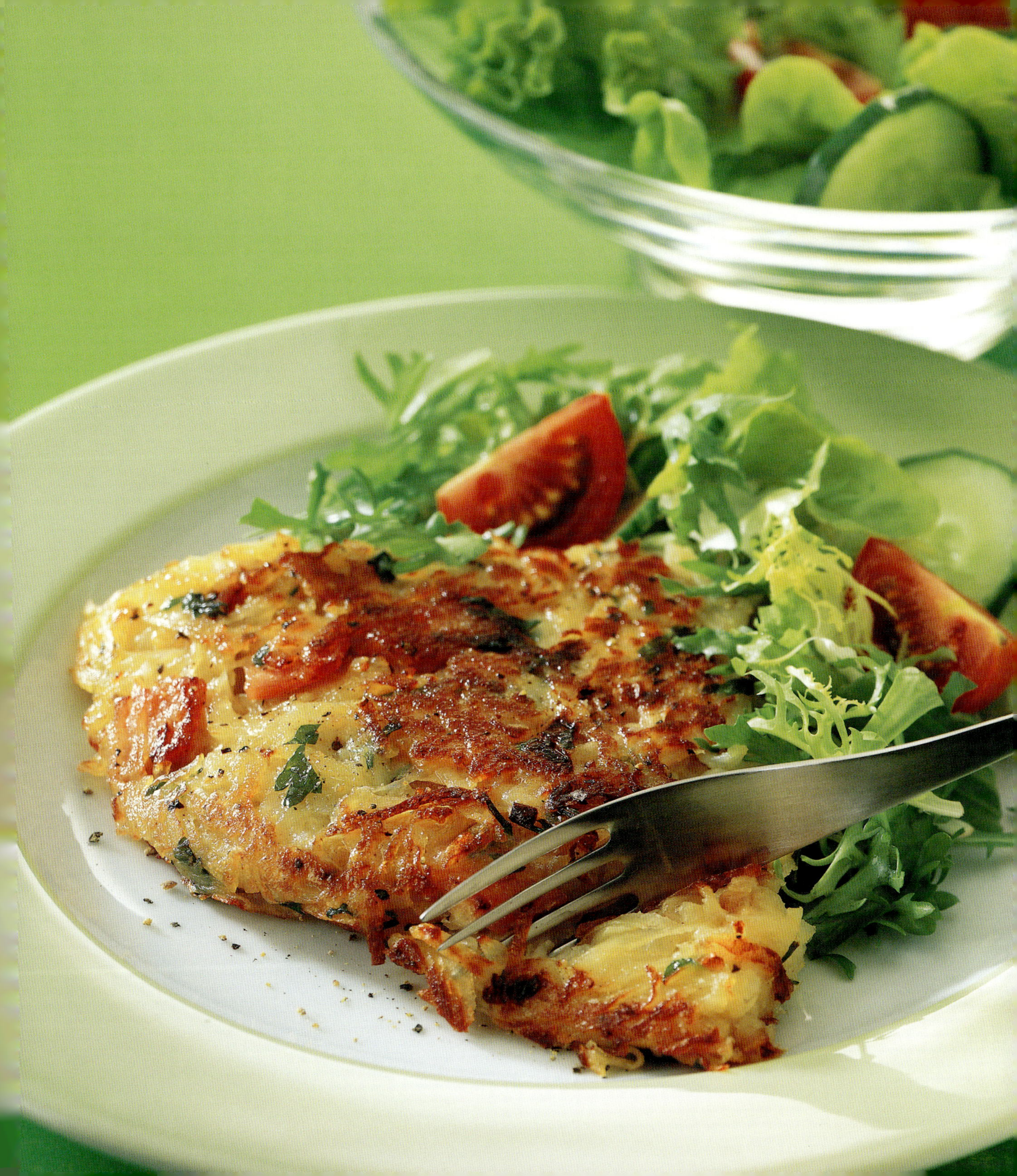

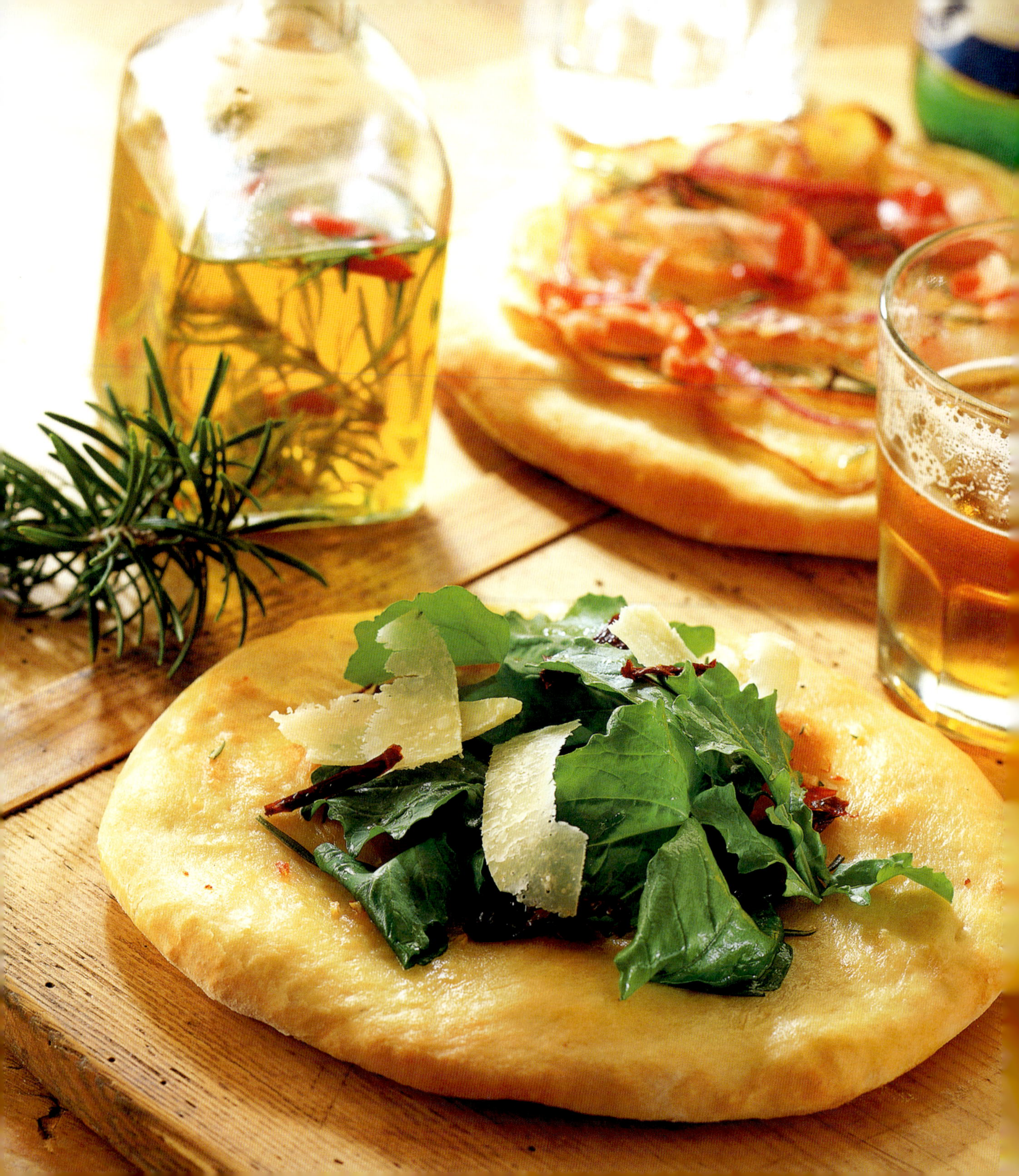

Potato and red onion pizza

FOR THE DOUGH
500 ml/17 fl oz/2 cups warm water
1 sachet dried yeast
1 teaspoon caster (superfine) sugar
1 kg/2¼ lb bread flour
1 tablespoon extra virgin olive oil
2 teaspoons sea salt

FOR THE TOPPING
2½ tablespoons chilli oil
4 potatoes, thinly sliced
2 small red onions, thinly sliced
3 sprigs rosemary, leaves removed and chopped
100 g/3½ oz rocket (arugula) leaves
45 g/1½ oz Parmesan, shaved

makes 8

To make the pizza dough, combine the warm water, yeast and sugar in a bowl. Add 400 g/14 oz of the flour, and stir until the mixture is a sloppy paste. Gradually add another 500 g/1 lb 2 oz of the flour, then the oil and salt, and work together with your hands until the mixture forms a ball. Knead the dough with your hands for 10 minutes until very elastic and smooth. Put in a clean bowl. Cover with a damp cloth and leave in a warm place for 2 hours, or until dough has doubled in size.

Preheat the oven to 240°C/475°F/Gas mark 9. Cut the dough into 8 equal pieces. Dust a baking sheet with flour. Dust the work surface with flour, take one piece of dough and press out with your hands to form a thick disc.

Roll out the dough in one direction, turn 90 degrees, and roll again in one direction, repeating this process until dough forms a 75 mm/3 in circle.

Place on the baking tray and brush with the chilli oil, then top with potato, onion and rosemary. Repeat with remaining dough and toppings, then bake for 5–10 minutes, or until brown. Top with rocket and Parmesan, drizzle with a little oil and serve.

Mains

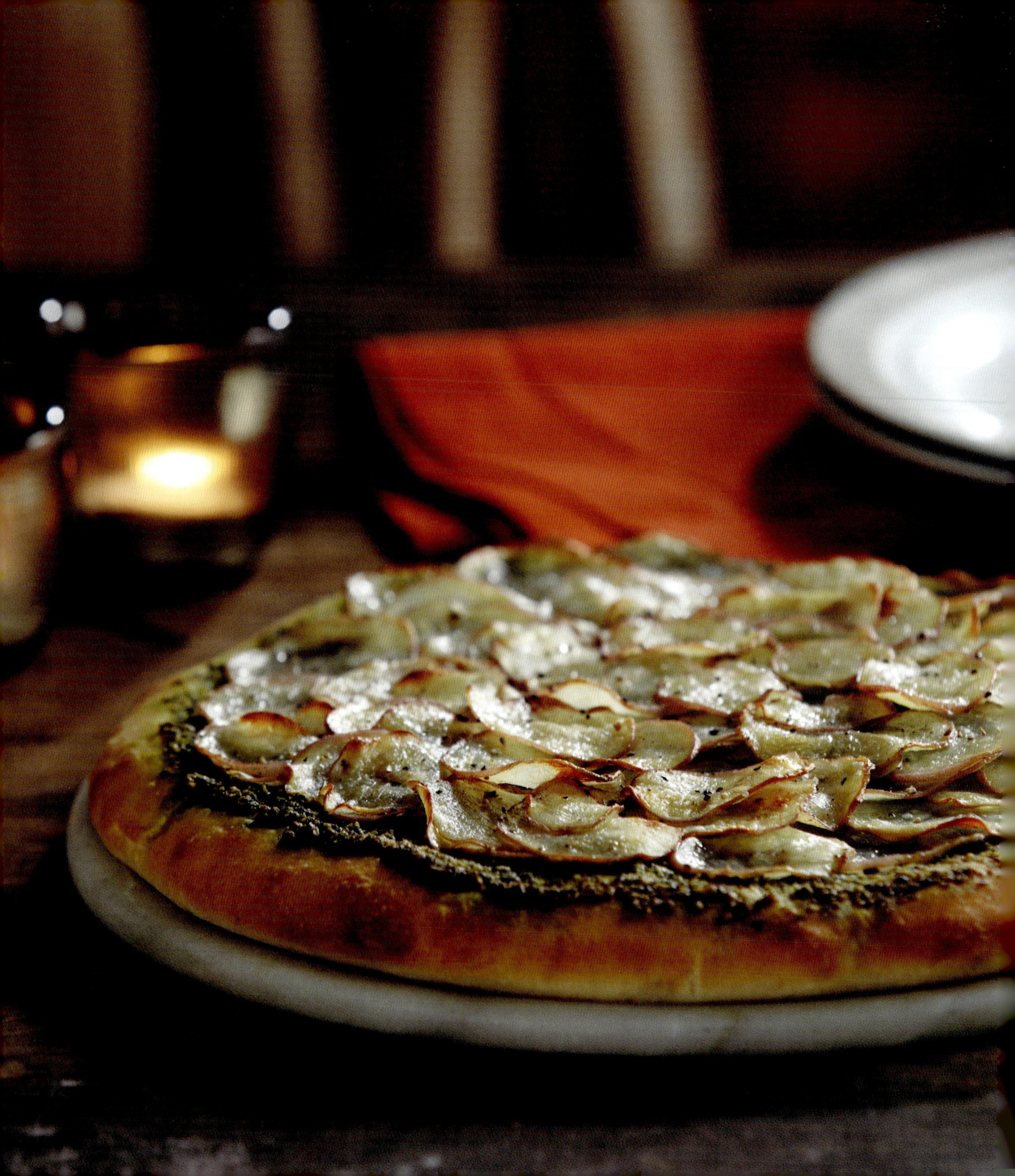

Roasted new potato pizza

1 teaspoon olive oil, plus 2 tablespoons
2 red-skinned new potatoes, thinly sliced
1 quantity basic pizza dough (see previous page)
½ cup spinach leaves, chopped
½ cup/4 tablespoons flat-leaf parsley, chopped
¼ cup/2 tablespoons fresh basil, chopped
2 garlic cloves, finely chopped
30 g/1 oz/¼ cup walnuts, coarsely chopped
30 g/1 oz/ Parmesan, grated
salt and freshly ground black pepper

makes 1

Preheat the oven to 230°C /450°F/Gas mark 8.

Lightly oil a baking sheet. Place the sliced potatoes in a bowl and sprinkle with salt, pepper and 1 teaspoon of oil. Toss well to coat evenly. Place on pthe repared baking sheet and roast until lightly browned, about 10 minutes.

Shape the pizza dough and place the spinach, parsley, basil, garlic, walnuts, 2 tablespoons olive oil and the Parmesan into a blender or food processor and purée. Spread the purée thickly on pizza dough. Place the roasted potatoes on top. Bake until lightly browned, about 15 minutes. Serve hot.

Roasted leg of lamb with vegetables

1 leg of lamb (about 1.5 kg/ 3 lb 5 oz)
2 garlic cloves, cut into slivers
2 fresh rosemary sprigs, cut into small pieces
400 g (14 oz) parsnips, chopped
300 g (10½ oz) carrots, chopped
6 heads chicory, cut into quarters lengthwise
310 ml/10 fl oz/1¼ cups red or white wine
2 tablespoons red wine vinegar
salt and black pepper

Preheat the oven to 180°C/350°F/Gas mark 4. Make several incisions in the lamb using a sharp knife. Push the garlic slivers and pieces of rosemary into the incisions, then season well.

Arrange the vegetables in a large roasting tin (pan) and place the lamb on top. Pour in the wine and vinegar and roast for 2–2½ hours until the lamb is tender, basting the lamb and turning the vegetables in the cooking juices every 30 minutes. Add a little more wine or water, if necessary.

Transfer the lamb to a plate, reserving the cooking juices, then cover with foil and rest for 15 minutes. Carve the lamb and serve with the vegetables, with the cooking juices drizzled over.

serves 4

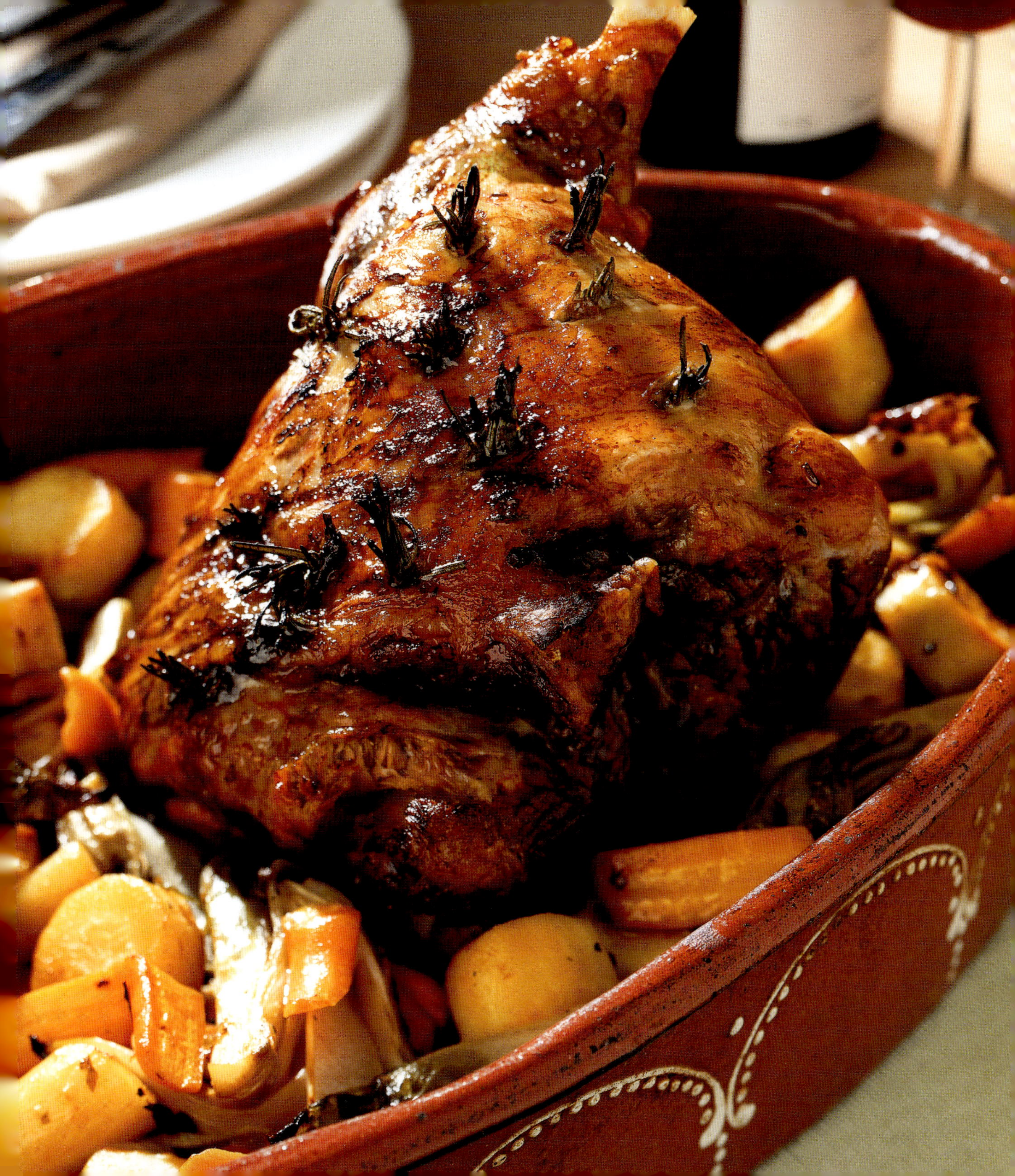

Root vegetable curry

1 tablespoon olive oil
1 onion, chopped
1 green chilli, deseeded and finely chopped
1 garlic clove, finely chopped
2.5 cm/1 in piece fresh root ginger, finely chopped
2 tablespoons plain (all-purpose) flour
2 teaspoons each ground coriander, ground cumin and turmeric
300 ml/½ pint vegetable stock
200 ml/7 fl oz tomato purée
750 g/1 lb 10 oz/ mixed root vegetables, cubed
2 carrots, thinly sliced
chopped fresh coriander (cilantro), to garnish
freshly ground black pepper
couscous, to serve

Heat the oil in a large saucepan. Add the onion, chilli, garlic and ginger and fry for 5 minutes, or until softened, stirring occasionally. Stir in the flour, ground coriander, cumin and turmeric and cook gently, stirring, for 1 minute to release the flavours.

Gradually stir in the stock, then add the tomato purée, cubed root vegetables and the carrots. Season with black pepper and mix well.

Bring to the boil, stirring, then cover, reduce the heat and simmer for 45 minutes or until the vegetables are tender, stirring occasionally. Garnish with fresh coriander and serve with couscous.

serves 4

Mains

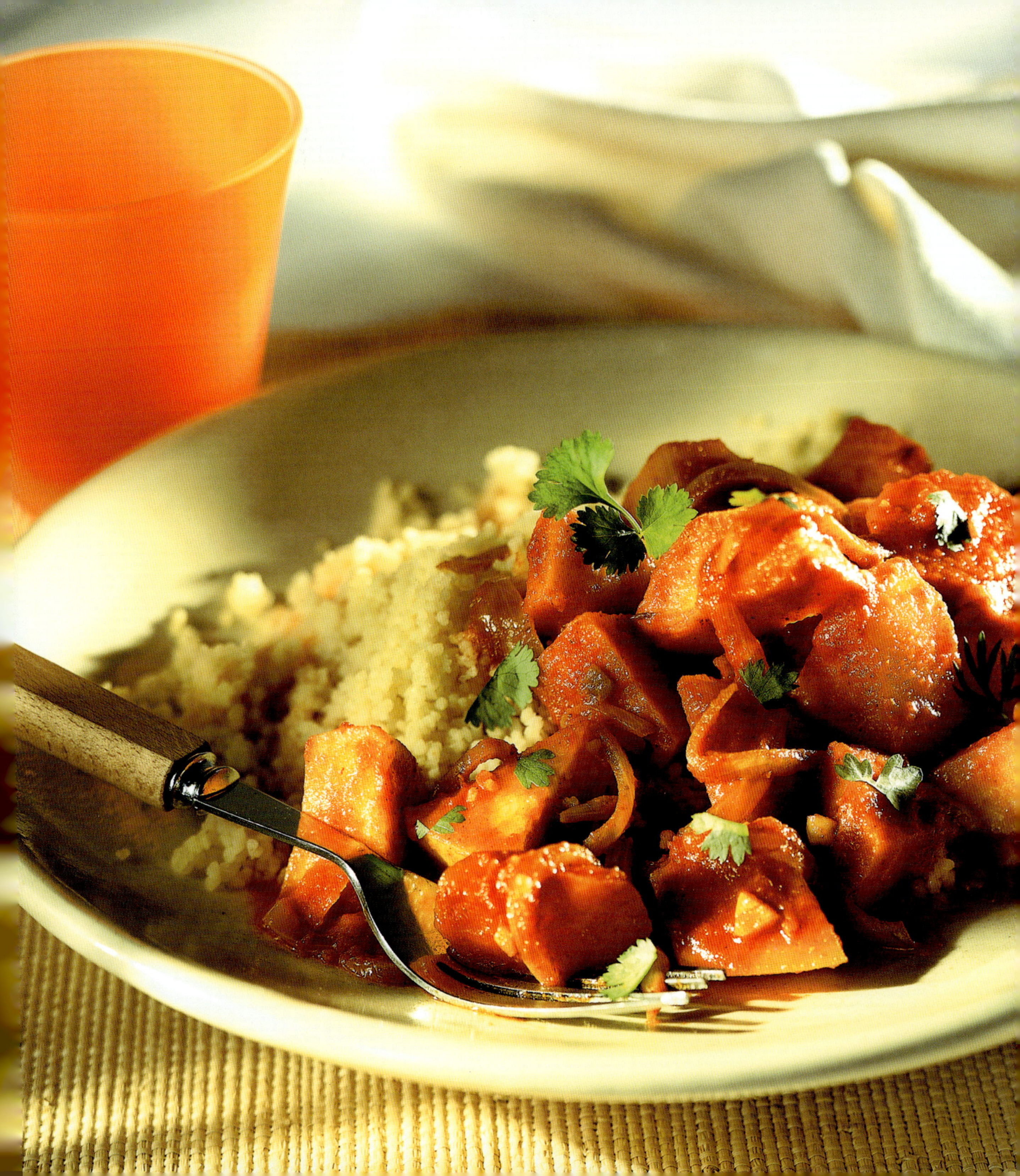

Sides

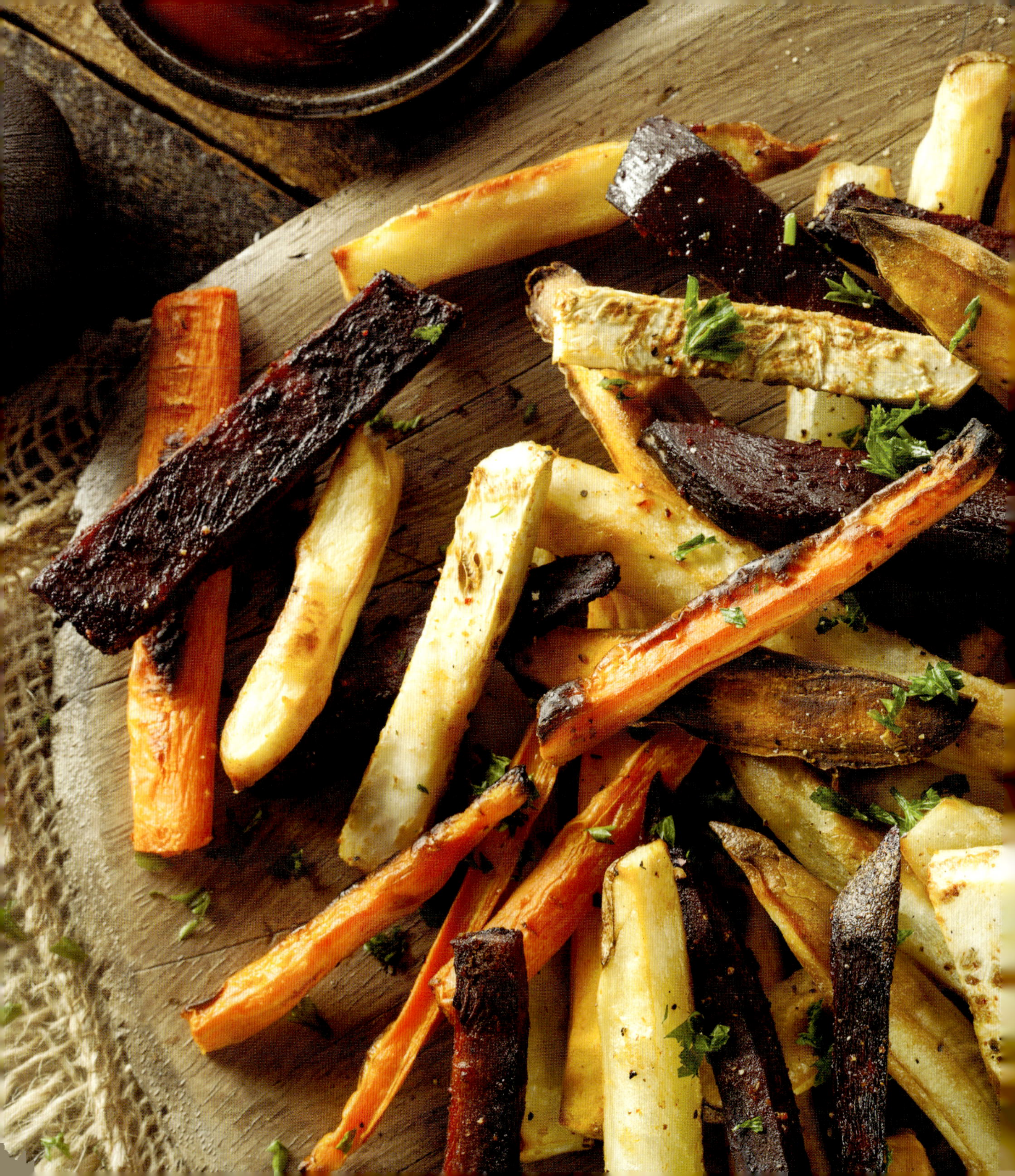

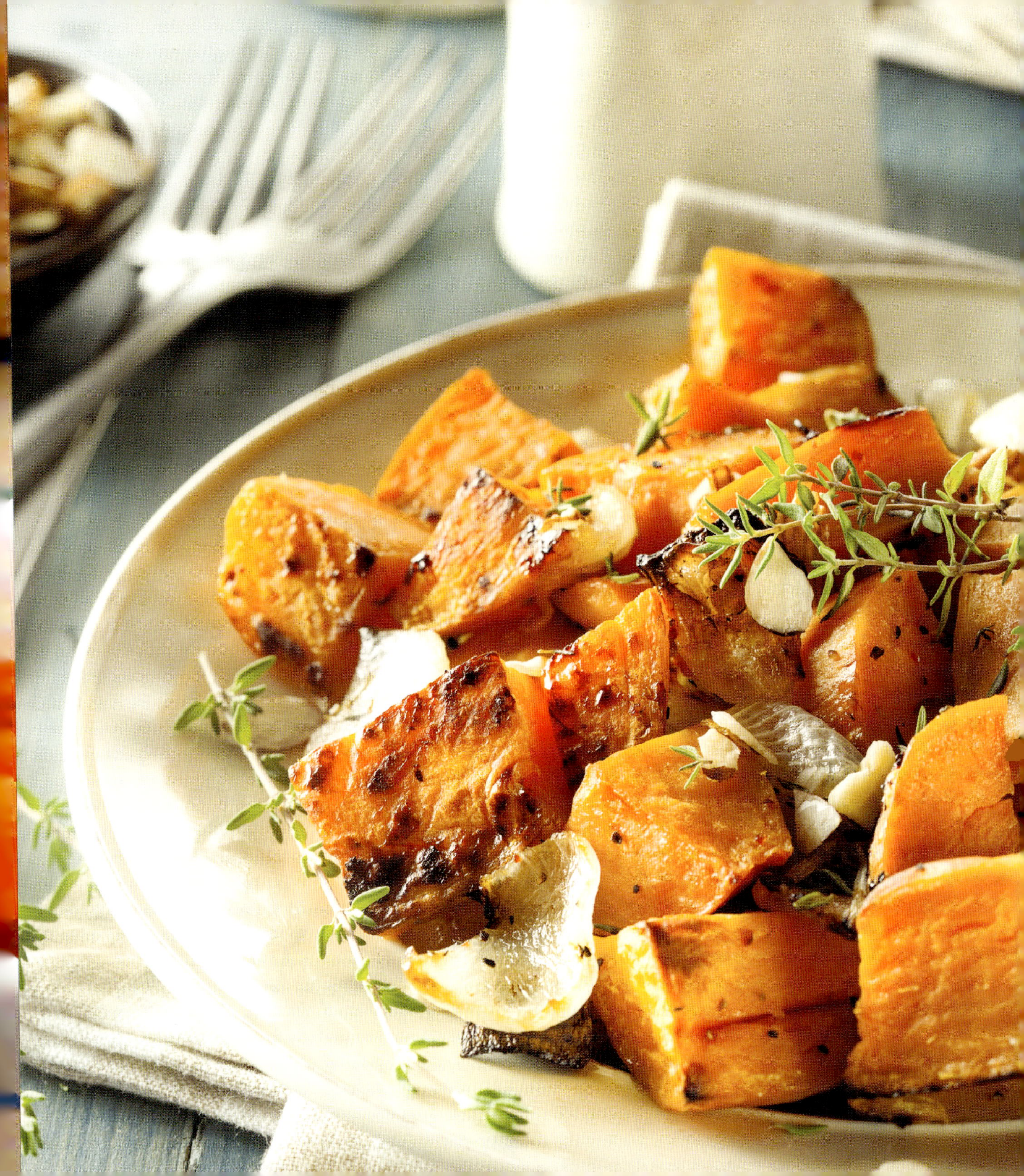

Spicy carrot salad

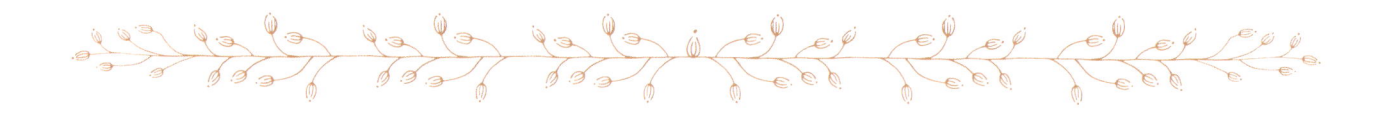

500 g/1 lb 2 oz baby carrots
2 tablespoons olive oil
juice of 1 lemon
½ teaspoon chilli powder
1 teaspoon ground cinnamon
1 teaspoon sugar
1 garlic clove, crushed
1 teaspoon salt
½ teaspoon ground ginger
parsley, to garnish

serves 4–6

Place the whole carrots in a saucepan, cover with water, bring to the boil and cook for about 20 minutes until soft. Set aside in their cooking water for about 1 hour.

When cool, strain the carrots and cut them into quarters lengthwise.

Return the carrots to the pan, cover with the rest of the ingredients and heat for a few minutes to blend the flavours.

Leave to cool. Serve garnished with freshly chopped parsley.

Sides

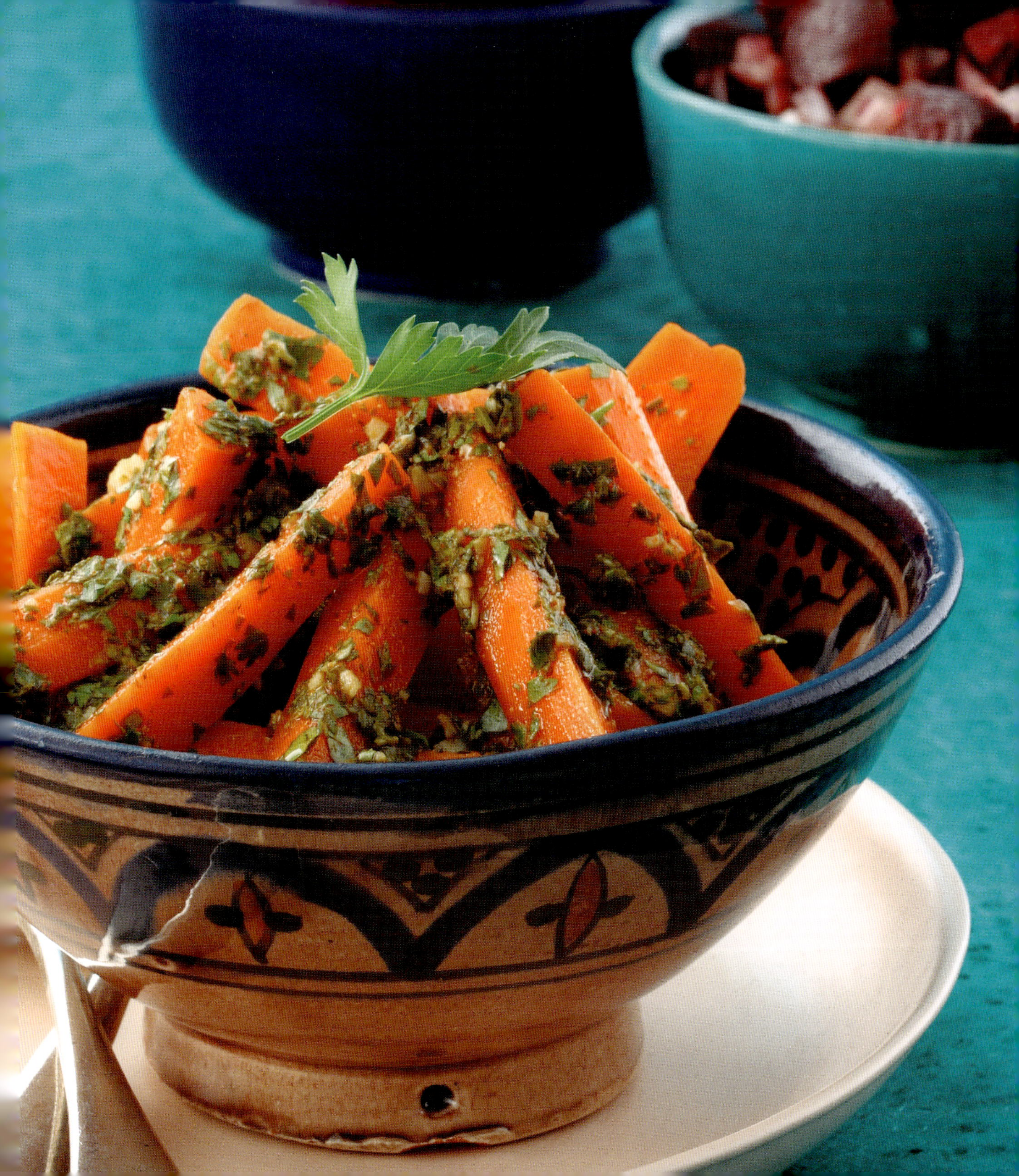

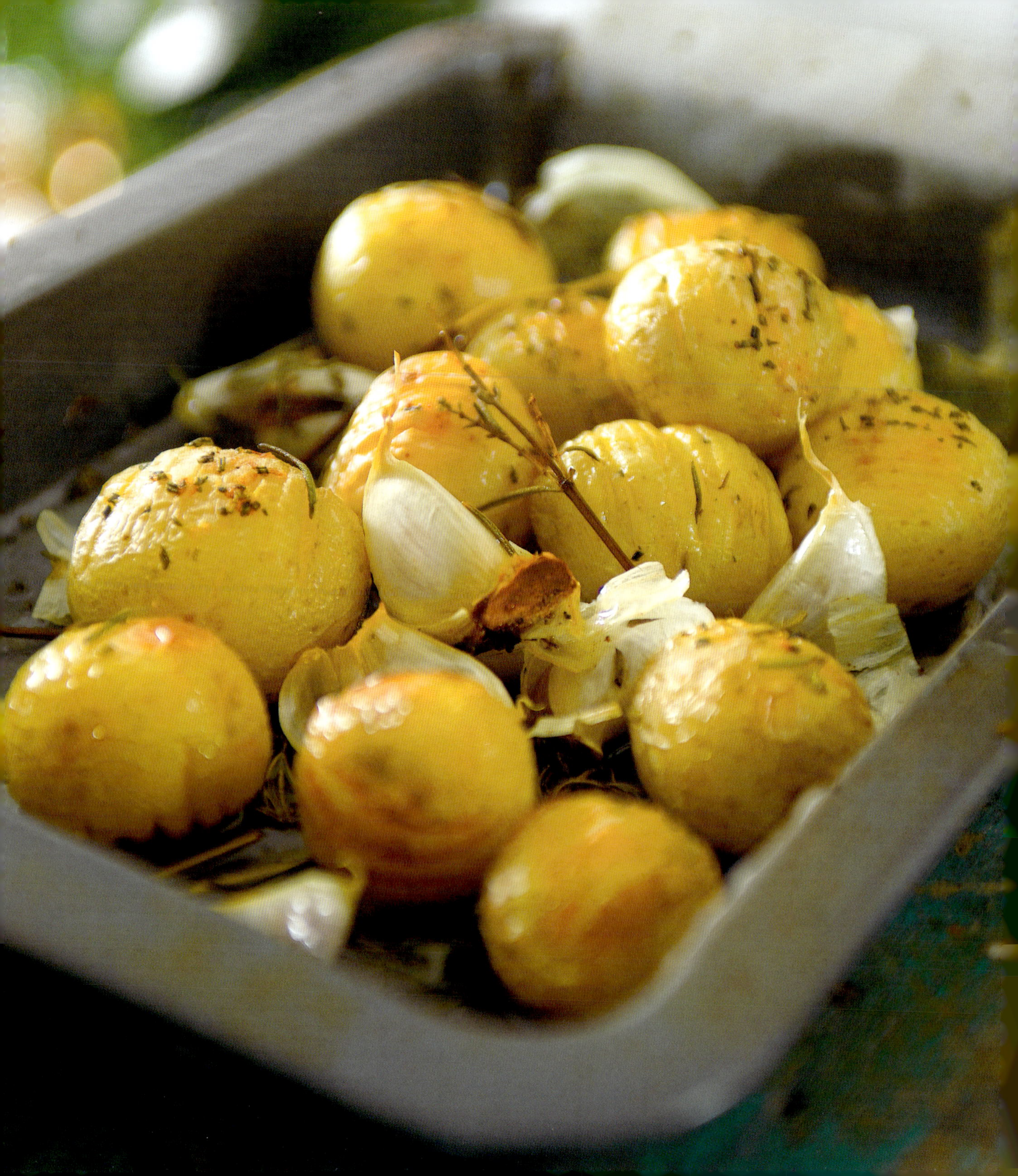

Roast potatoes with garlic and rosemary

1.5 kg/3 lb 5 oz chat potatoes
1 bulb garlic
6 sprigs rosemary, leaves removed and chopped
6 tablespoons olive oil
coarse sea salt

serves 8

Preheat the oven to 190°C/375°F/Gas mark 5. Place the potatoes in a large pan, cover with water, add salt and bring to the boil. Reduce the heat and simmer for 2 minutes, then drain well. When cool enough to handle, make a few slashes across the tops of the potatoes. Break open the garlic and discard any loose pieces of skin.

Place the potatoes and garlic cloves in a roasting dish, sprinkle with the chopped rosemary and oil. Bake for about 1¼ hours, turning occasionally, until crisp and golden brown.

Transfer to a warmed serving dish, sprinkle with salt and garnish with extra rosemary sprigs.

Sides

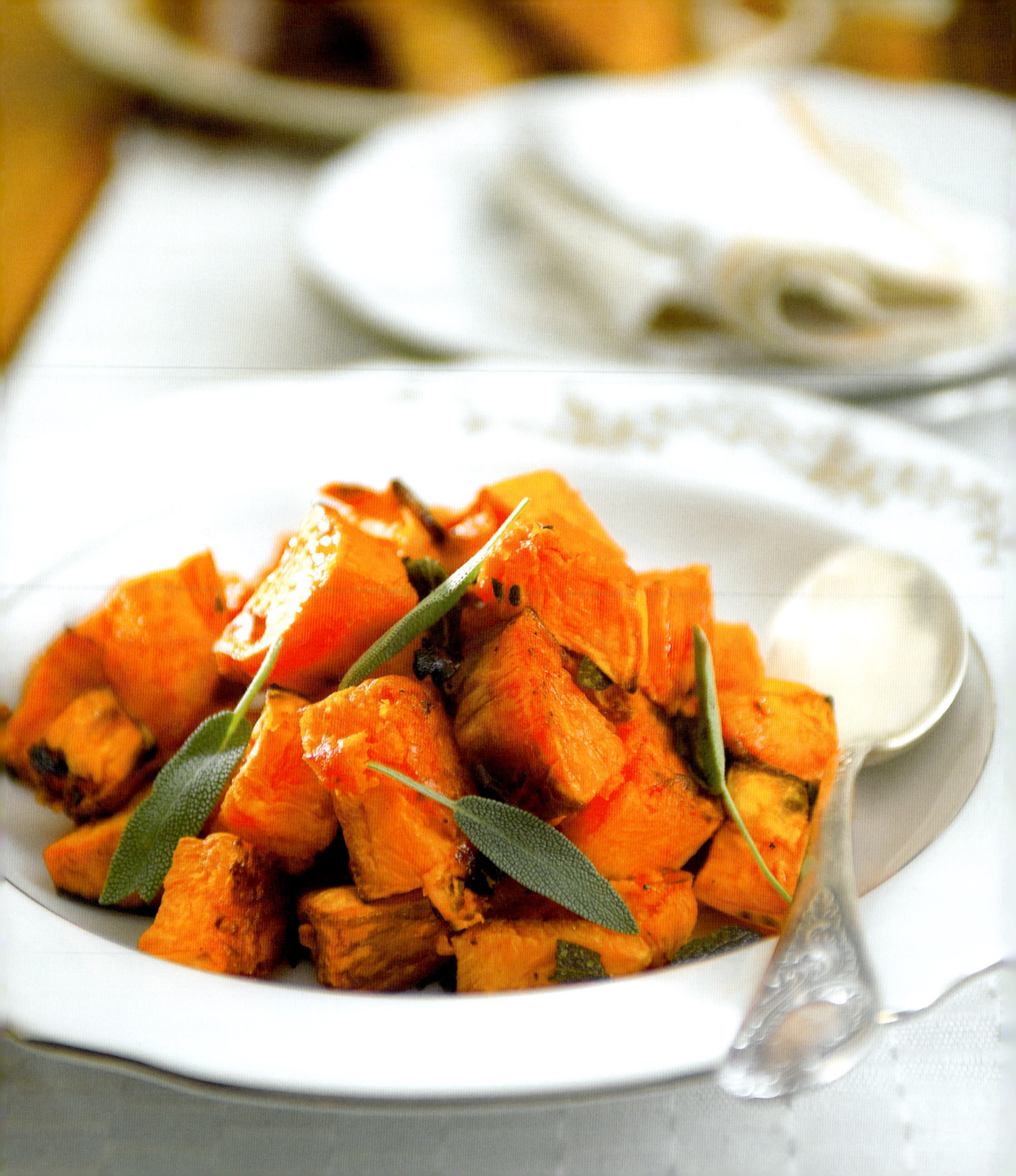

Sweet potatoes with sage

1 kg/2¼ lb sweet potatoes, peeled and cut into even pieces
30 g/1 oz butter
2 tablespoon vegetable oil
1½ tablespoons honey
pinch of ground ginger
6 fresh sage leaves, torn into pieces
salt

serves 8

Preheat the oven to 180°C/350°F/Gas mark 4.

Cook the sweet potatoes in a large pan of boiling salted water for 5 minutes. Drain.

Melt the butter with the oil in a baking dish and stir in the honey and ginger. Add the sage and the sweet potatoes and toss in the mixture to coat.

Bake for 40 minutes, brushing with honey mixture and turning occasionally, until the potatoes are tender. Garnish with extra sage.

Potato and tomato bake

750 ml/25 fl oz/3 cups vegetable stock
750 g/1 lb 10 oz potatoes, peeled and thinly sliced
1 red bell pepper (capsicum)
butter, for greasing
6 Roma tomatoes, sliced
2 tablespoons lemon juice
2 tablespoons olive oil
¼ teaspoon sugar
¼ small bunch flat-leaf parsley, chopped
¼ small bunch coriander (cilantro), chopped
freshly ground black pepper

serves 4

Heat the vegetable stock in a large frying pan set over medium heat. Add the potatoes and cook for 8–10 minutes, or until tender. Drain the potatoes, reserving 125 ml/4 fl oz/½ cup stock.

Meanwhile, cut the pepper into four and remove the seeds. Place on a grill (broiler) pan and bake under a hot grill for 6-8 minutes, or until the skin blisters. Leave to cool then remove the skin and slice thinly.

Preheat the oven to 220°C/425°F/Gas mark 8. Lightly butter a shallow casserole dish.

Arrange the potato slices and pepper in the casserole dish. Pour over the reserved stock and arrange the tomato slices on top. Drizzle with lemon juice and olive oil, then sprinkle with sugar and season with pepper.

Bake for 20 minutes, or until tomatoes are cooked. Garnish with parsley and cilantro to serve.

NOTE: Suitable for vegetarians, vegans and wheat allergy sufferers.

Sides

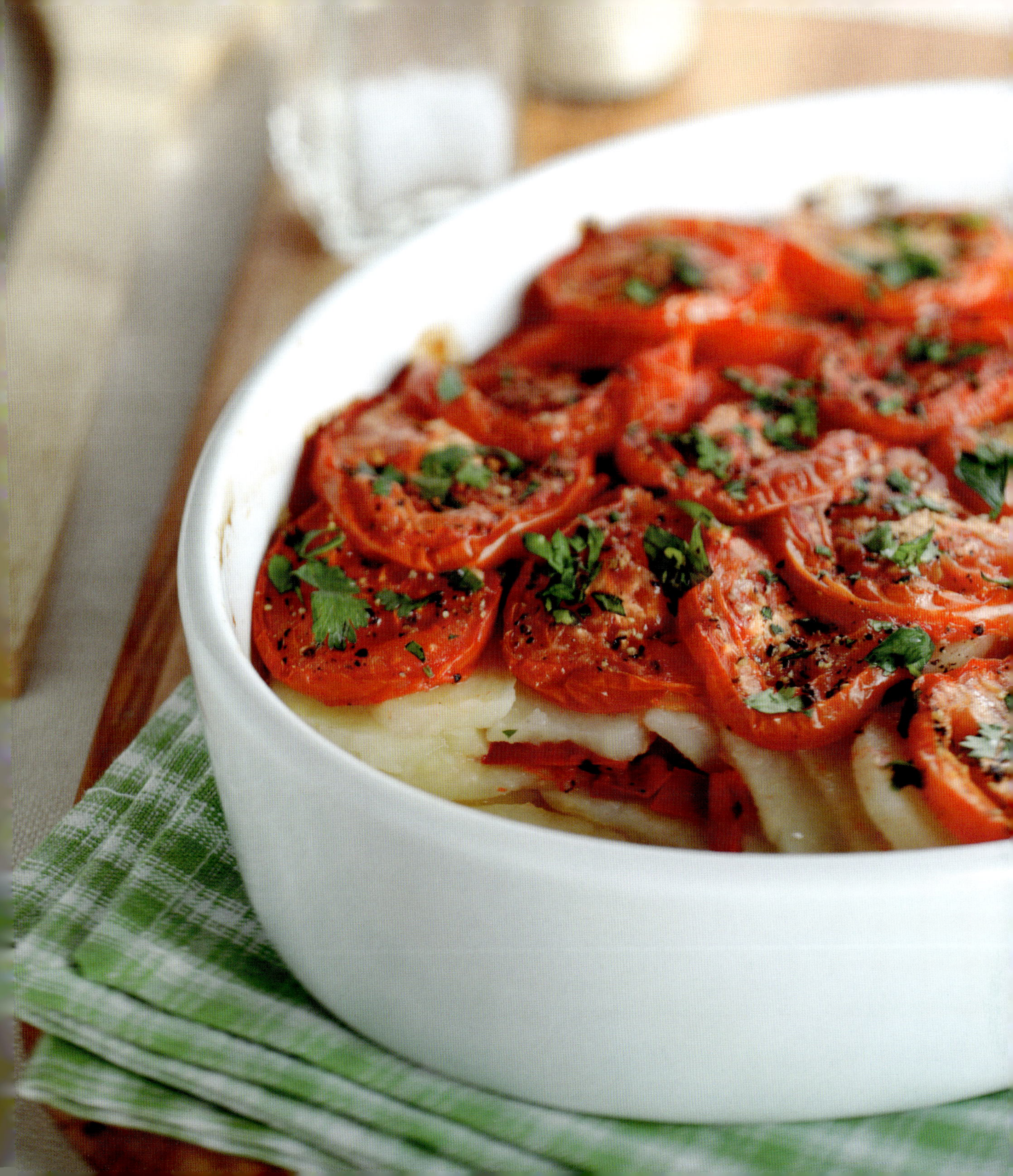

Warm herbed potato salad

1.4 kg/3 lb russet or Idaho potatoes, washed but not peeled
2 tablespoons olive oil
4 white onions, sliced
¼ cup/2 tablespoons dill, chopped
¼ cup/2 tablespoons chervil, chopped
¼ cup/2 tablespoons Italian parsley, chopped
zest of 1 lemon

165 ml/5½ fl oz/⅔ cup extra virgin olive oil
165 ml/5½ fl oz/⅔ cup white wine vinegar
juice of 1 lemon
3 garlic cloves
salt and freshly ground pepper

Cut the potatoes into large chunks, place in a saucepan, and boil in salted water for 10 minutes, or until tender but not soft.

In a heavy skillet, heat the oil and sauté the onions over a high heat until golden, about 8 minutes. Reduce the heat, cover, and cook slowly for 20 minutes until caremelized.

Drain the potatoes and return to the saucepan

In a small bowl, whisk the dressing ingredients until thickened. Pour the dressing over the hot potatoes and toss, adding the fresh herbs and lemon zest with salt and lots of pepper to taste.

Add the caramelised onions and toss thoroughly.

serves 6–8

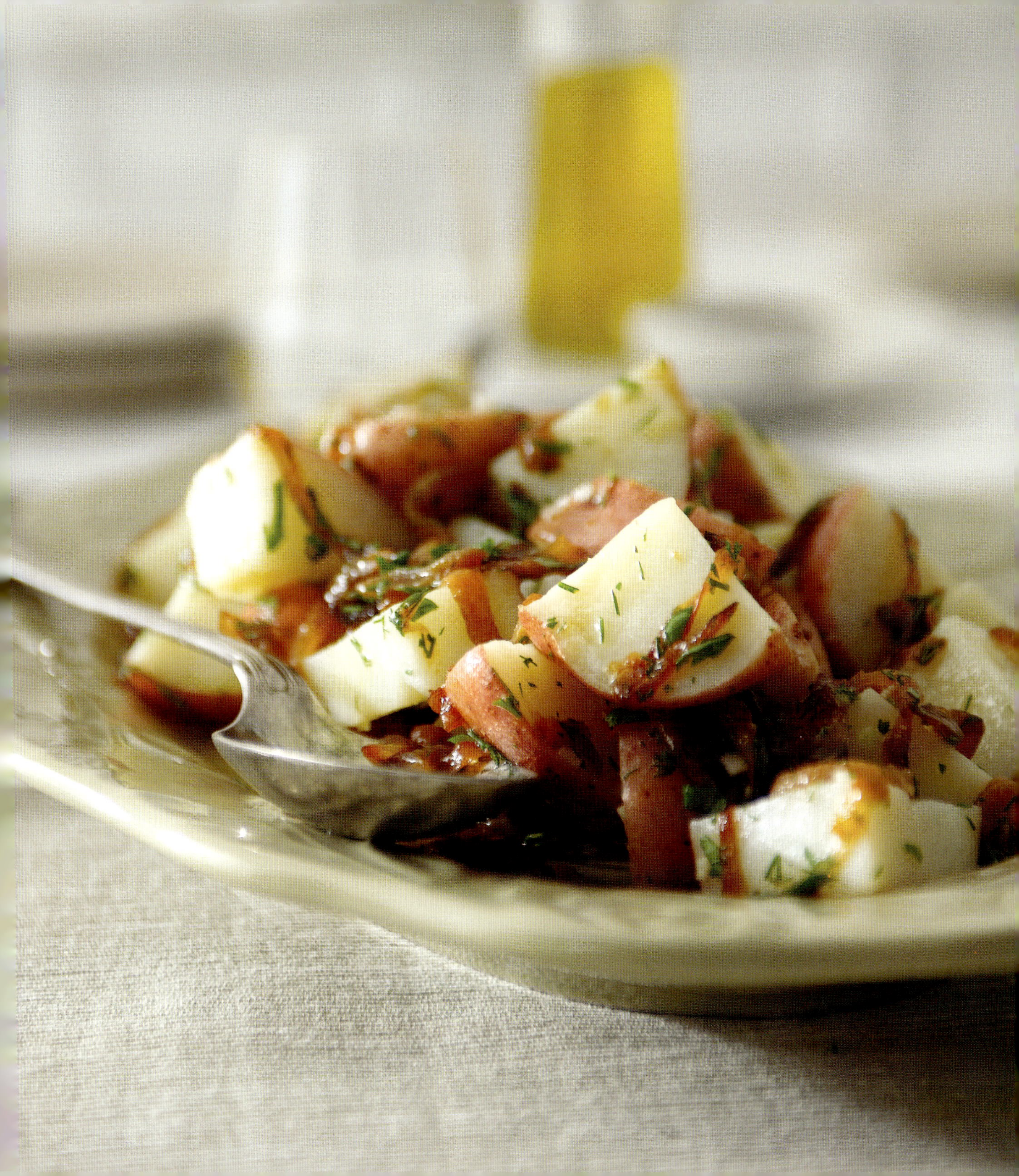

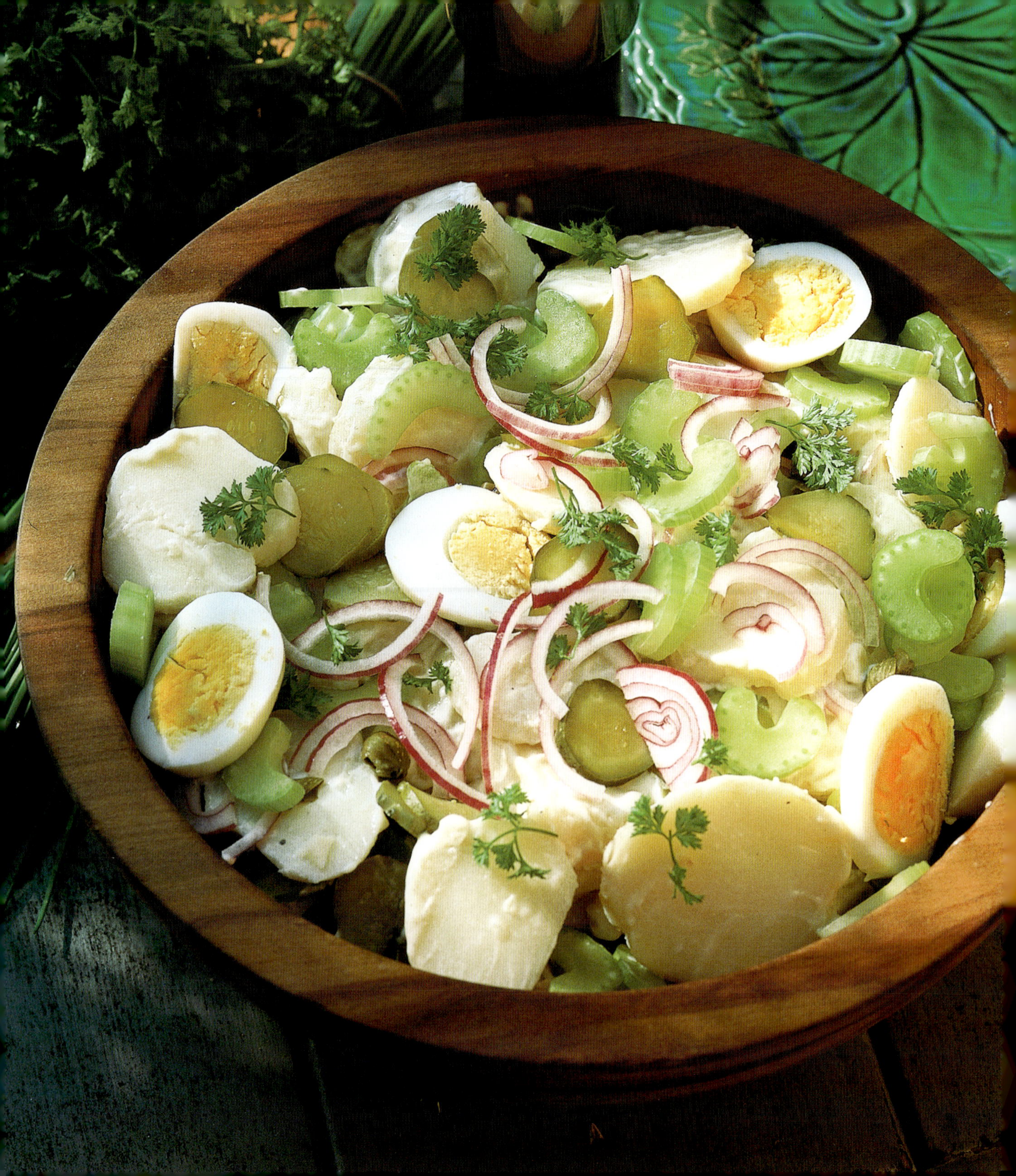

Classic potato salad

1 kg/2¼ lb new potatoes
75 ml/2½ fl oz/⅓ cup dry white wine
125 ml/4 fl oz/½ cup vinaigrette dressing
125 ml/4 fl oz/½ cup mayonnaise
1 red onion, sliced into rings
1 stalk celery, sliced
2 dill pickles or gherkins, thinly sliced
1 teaspoon capers
4 hard-boiled eggs, peeled and sliced
¼ cup/2 tablespoons parsley, chopped
salt and freshly ground black pepper

Scrub and boil the potatoes in salted water until tender. Peel and slice them while still hot and place into a bowl.

Drizzle with wine, turning the potato slices carefully. Next, drizzle with the vinaigrette dressing, then stir in the mayonnaise.

Toss with the remaining ingredients. Season with salt and pepper to serve.

serves 4

Sides

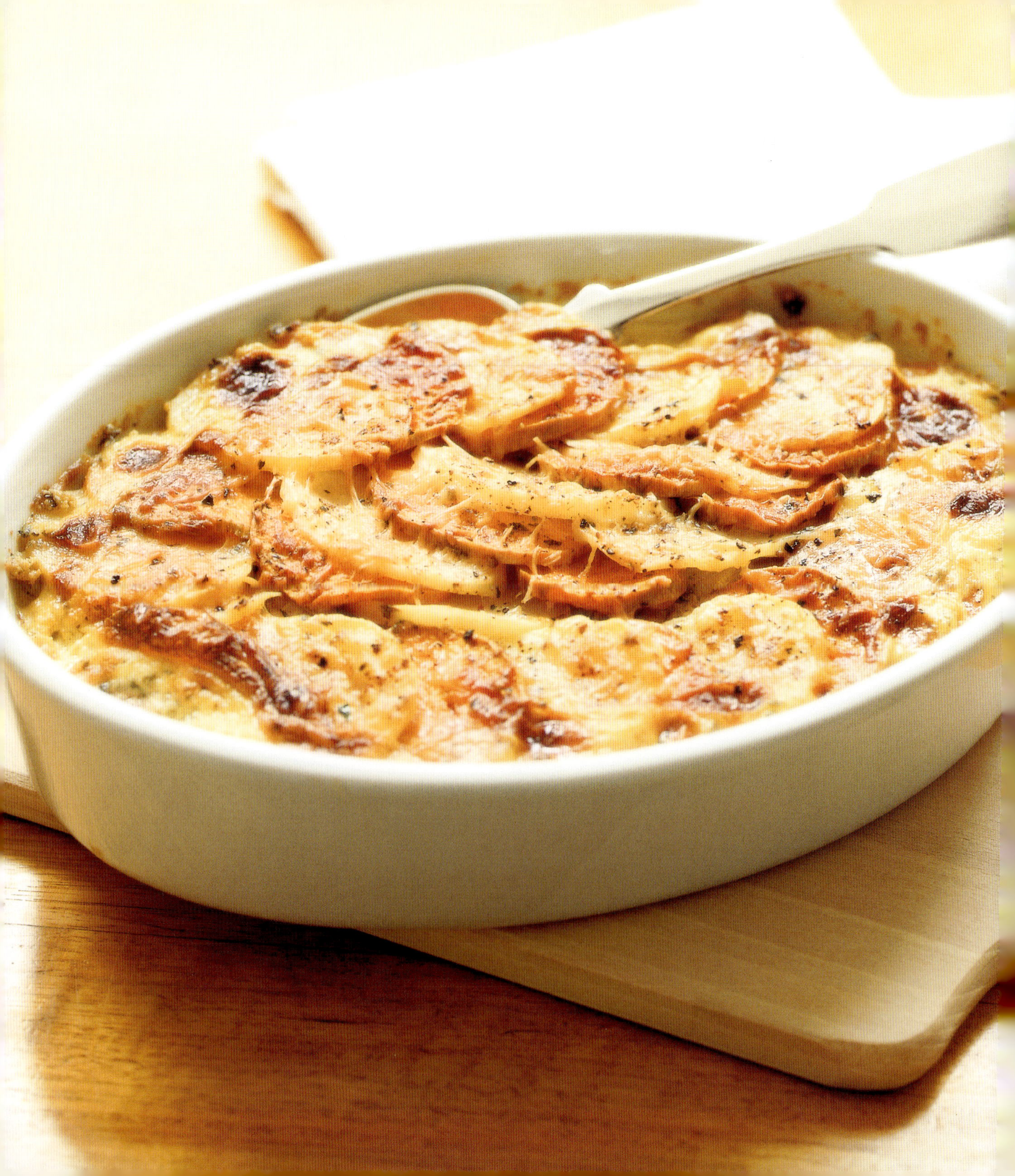

Potato and sweet potato creamy bake

2 tablespoons butter
2 leeks, trimmed, halved and sliced
1 kg/2¼ lb potatoes, peeled and thinly sliced
600 g/1 lb 6 oz sweet potato, peeled and thinly sliced
500 ml/17 fl oz/2 cups light (single) cream
1 teaspoon dried oregano
1 teaspoon dried basil
¼ teaspoon dried garlic granules
125 ml/½ cup chicken stock
3 tablespoons Parmesan, grated
¼ teaspoon nutmeg, ground
freshly ground black pepper
barbecued meat, to serve

serves 6–8

Preheat the oven to 200°C/400°F/Gas mark 6. Lightly grease an 18 x 25 cm/7 x 10 in baking dish.

Heat the butter in a frying pan. Add the leeks and cook for 3–4 minutes, or until soft.

Layer half the potatoes and sweet potatoes in the baking dish. Top with the leeks and layer with the remaining potato and sweet potato.

Combine the cream, oregano, basil, garlic granules and chicken stock in a large jug. Pour over the potatoes. Sprinkle with Parmesan, nutmeg and pepper.

Bake oven for 1–1½ hours or until the potatoes are tender. Cover with foil if the top starts to brown too much. Serve the bake with barbecued meats.

NOTE: The best potatoes for this dish are desiree, sebago or pontiac.

Sides

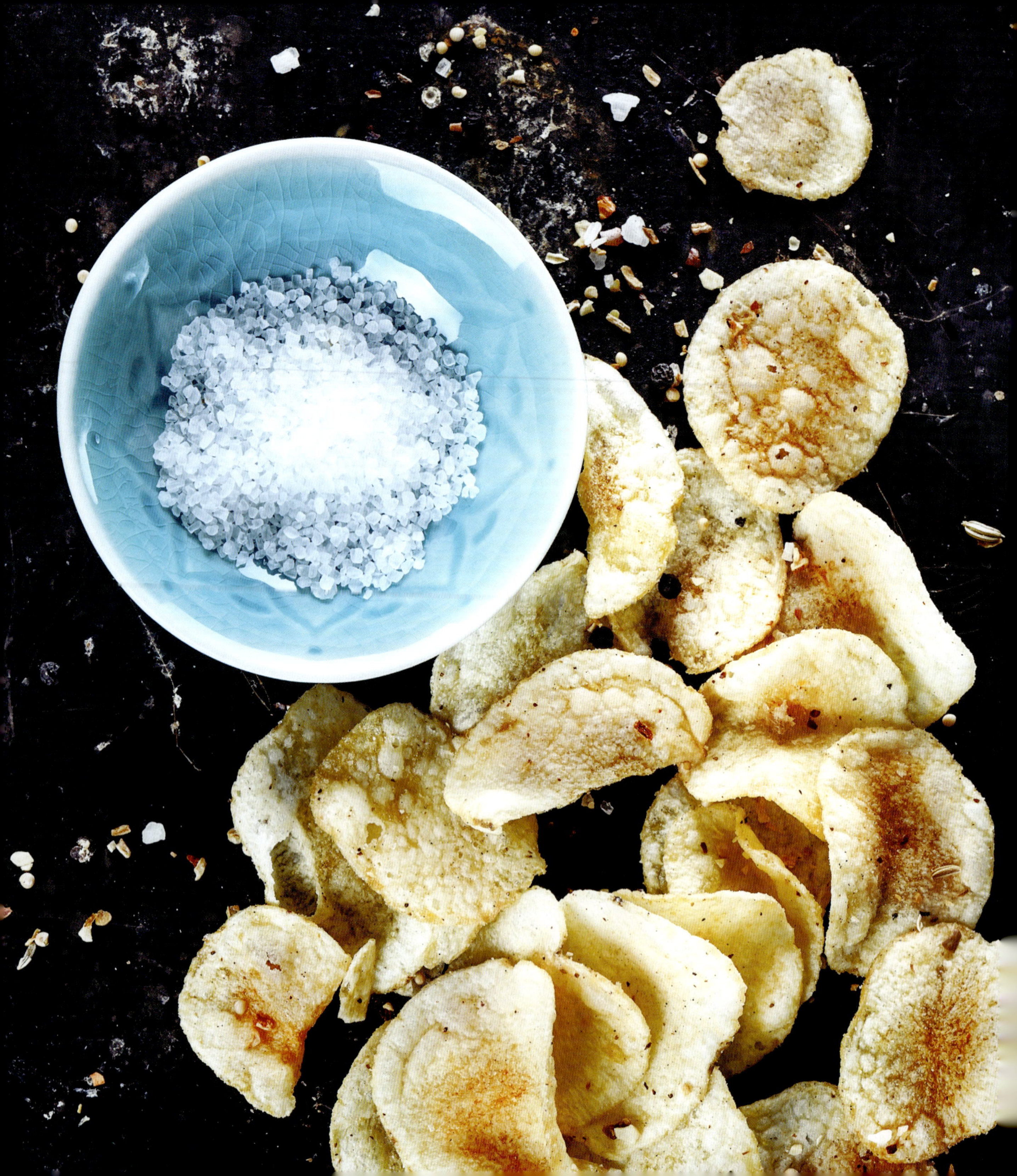

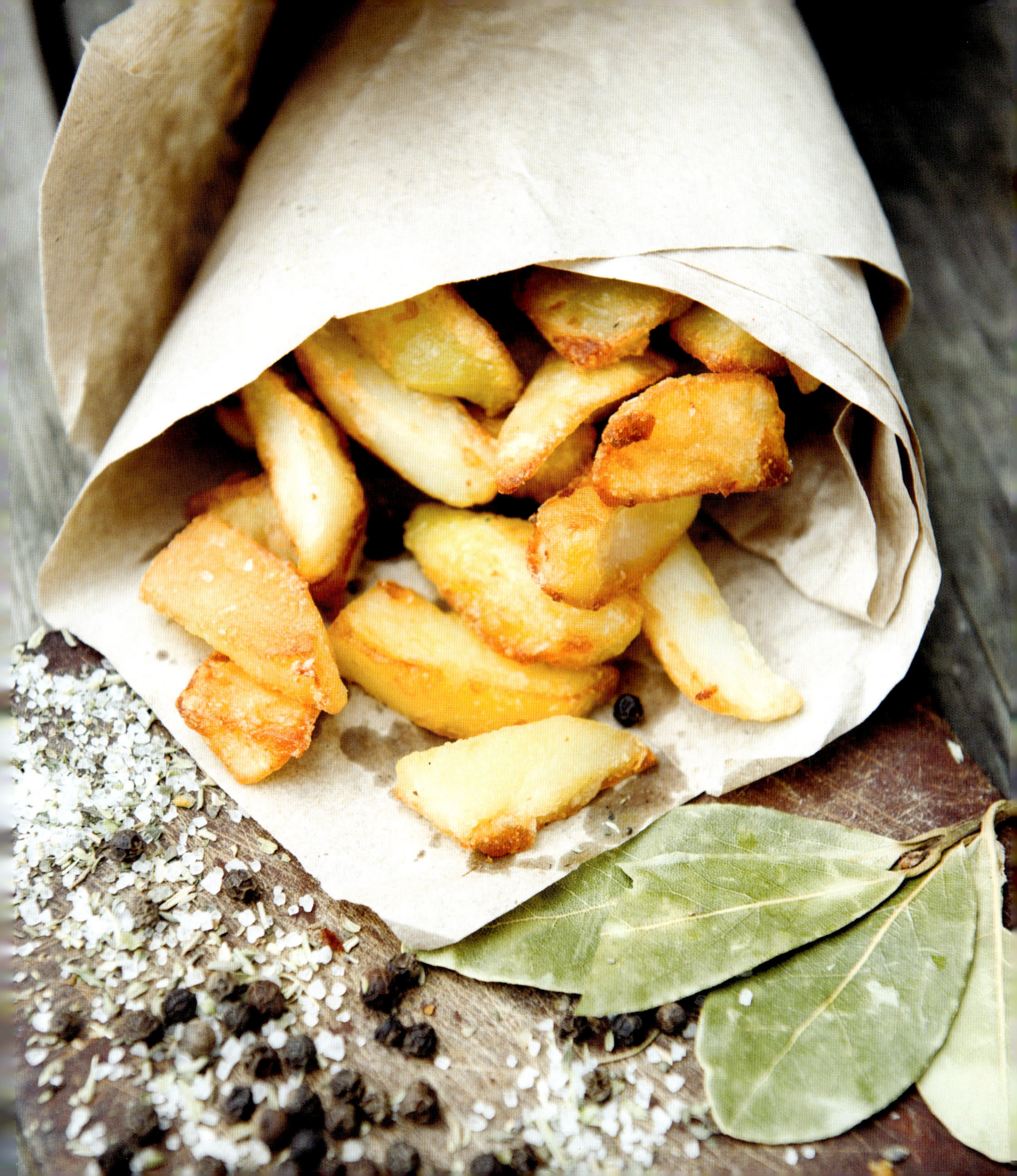

Carrots and snowpeas with sesame seeds

½ cucumber
2 tablespoons sesame seeds
1 tablespoon sunflower oil
4 carrots, cut into matchsticks
225 g/8 oz snowpeas (mange tout)
6 spring onions (scallions), chopped
1 tablespoon lemon juice
freshly ground black pepper

serves 4

Peel the cucumber, cut it in half lengthwise and scoop out the seeds. Slice into half moons.

Heat a non-stick wok or large frying pan. Add the sesame seeds and dry-fry for 1 minute or until toasted, tossing constantly. Remove and set aside. Add the oil, then the cucumber and carrots and stir-fry over a high heat for 2 minutes. Add the snowpeas and spring onions and stir-fry for another 2–3 minutes, until all the vegetables are cooked but still crisp.

Sprinkle over the lemon juice and sesame seeds, toss to mix and stir-fry for a few seconds to heat through. Season with pepper and serve.

Sides

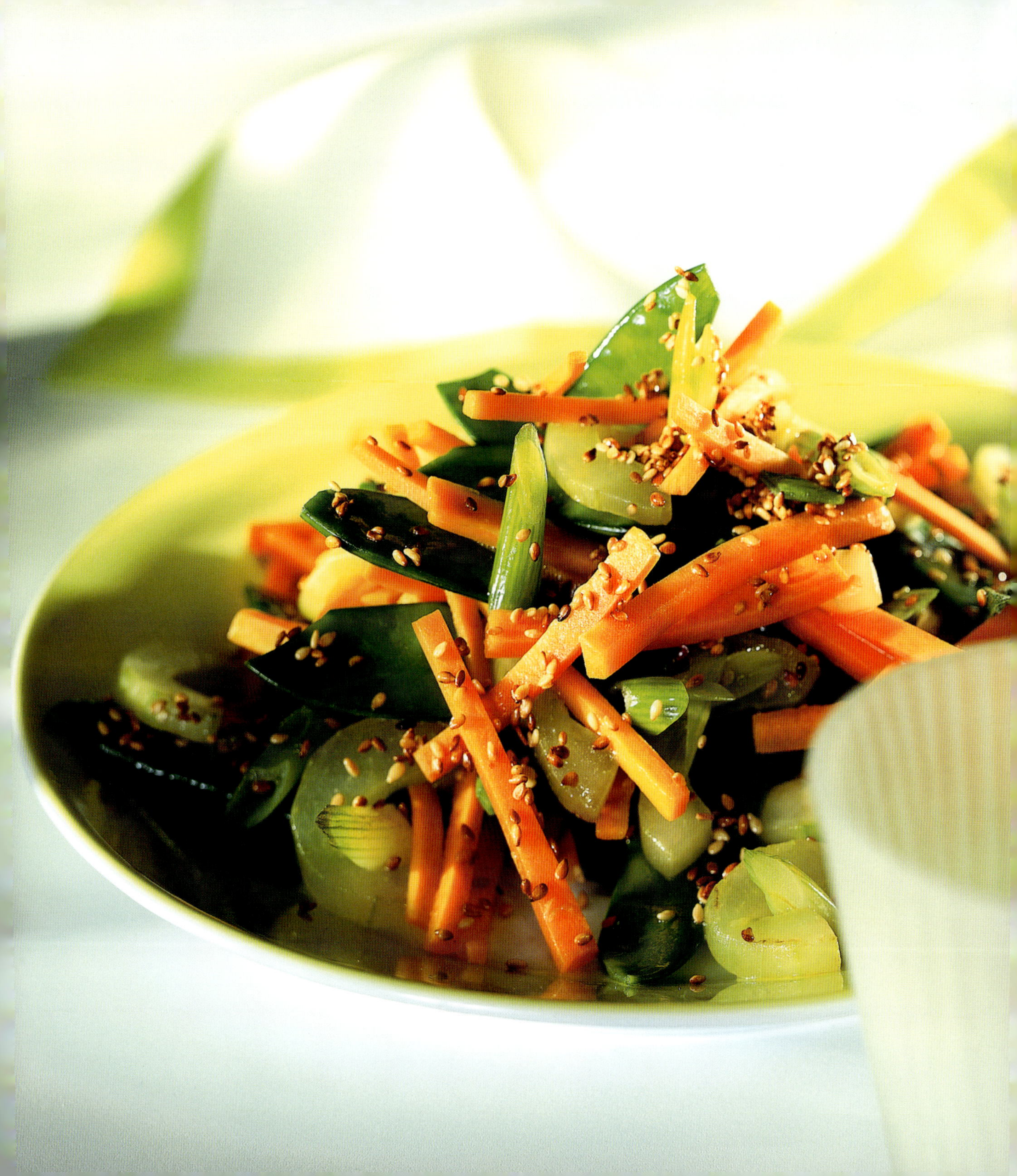

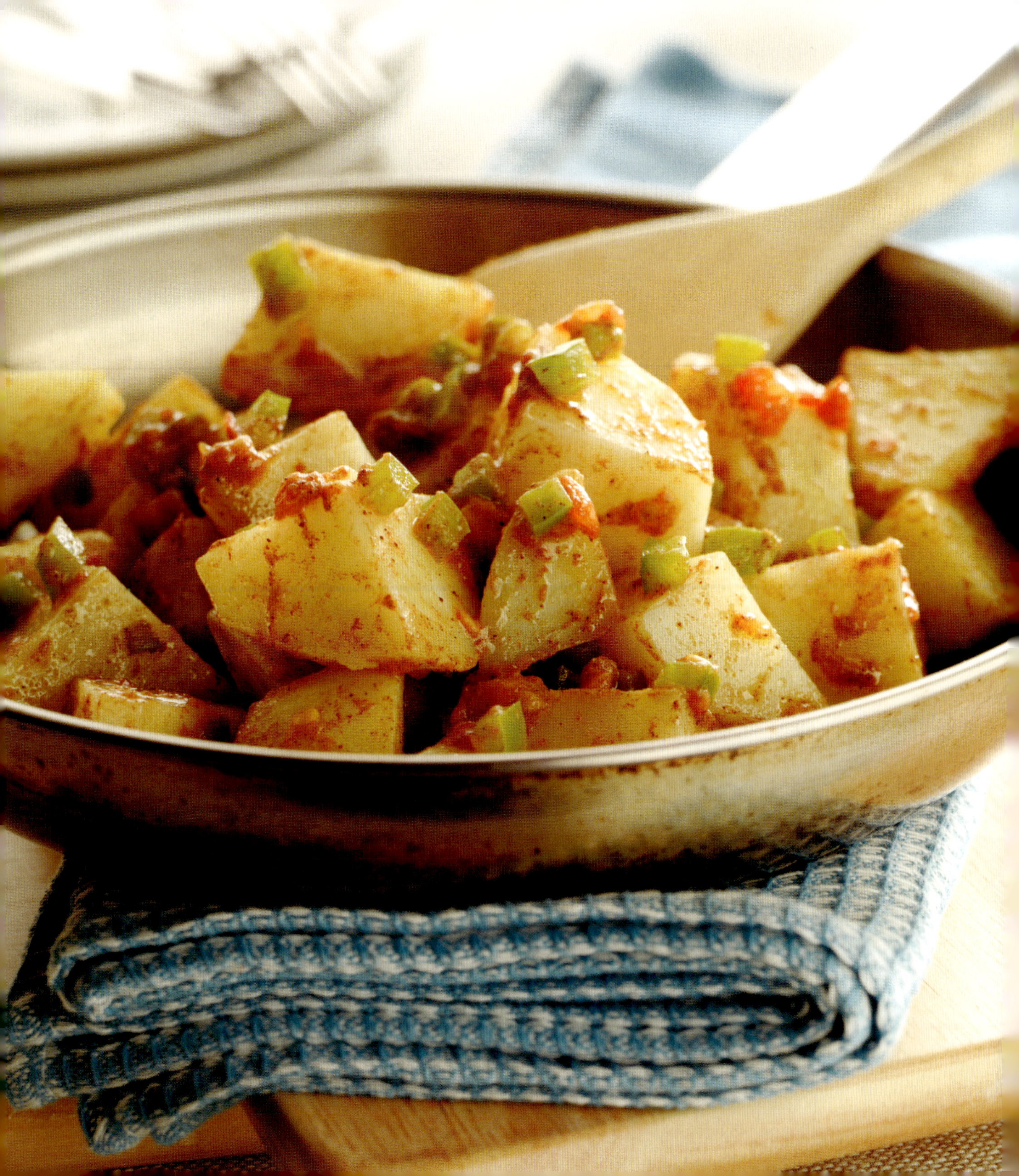

Spiced potatoes

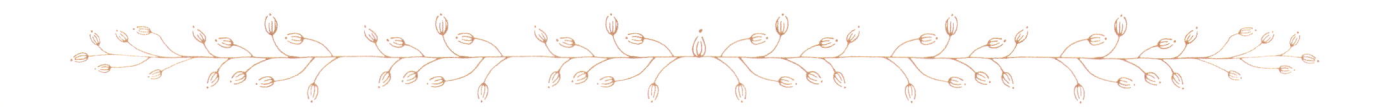

8 large Pontiac potatoes
3 tablespoons vegetable oil
½ teaspoon dry mustard
¼ teaspoon cayenne pepper
¼ teaspoon turmeric
¼ teaspoon allspice
½ teaspoon cinnamon
¼ teaspoon ginger
¼ teaspoon ground coriander
¼–½ teaspoon salt
1 teaspoon sugar
1 green capsicum (bell pepper), finely diced
2 Roma tomatoes, finely diced

serves 8

Peel the potatoes and cut into large chunks. Boil the potatoes for about 10 minutes until tender but firm.

In a frying pan, heat the oil and add the dry mustard, cayenne, turmeric, allspice, cinnamon, ginger, coriander, salt and sugar and cook for 1–2 minutes to release the fragrance of the spices. Add the green capsicum and tomatoes and cook for about 3 minutes, or until soft.

Add the potato chunks and cook over medium heat for about 8 minutes, or until they are very hot and have been entirely coated with the spice mixture.

Sides

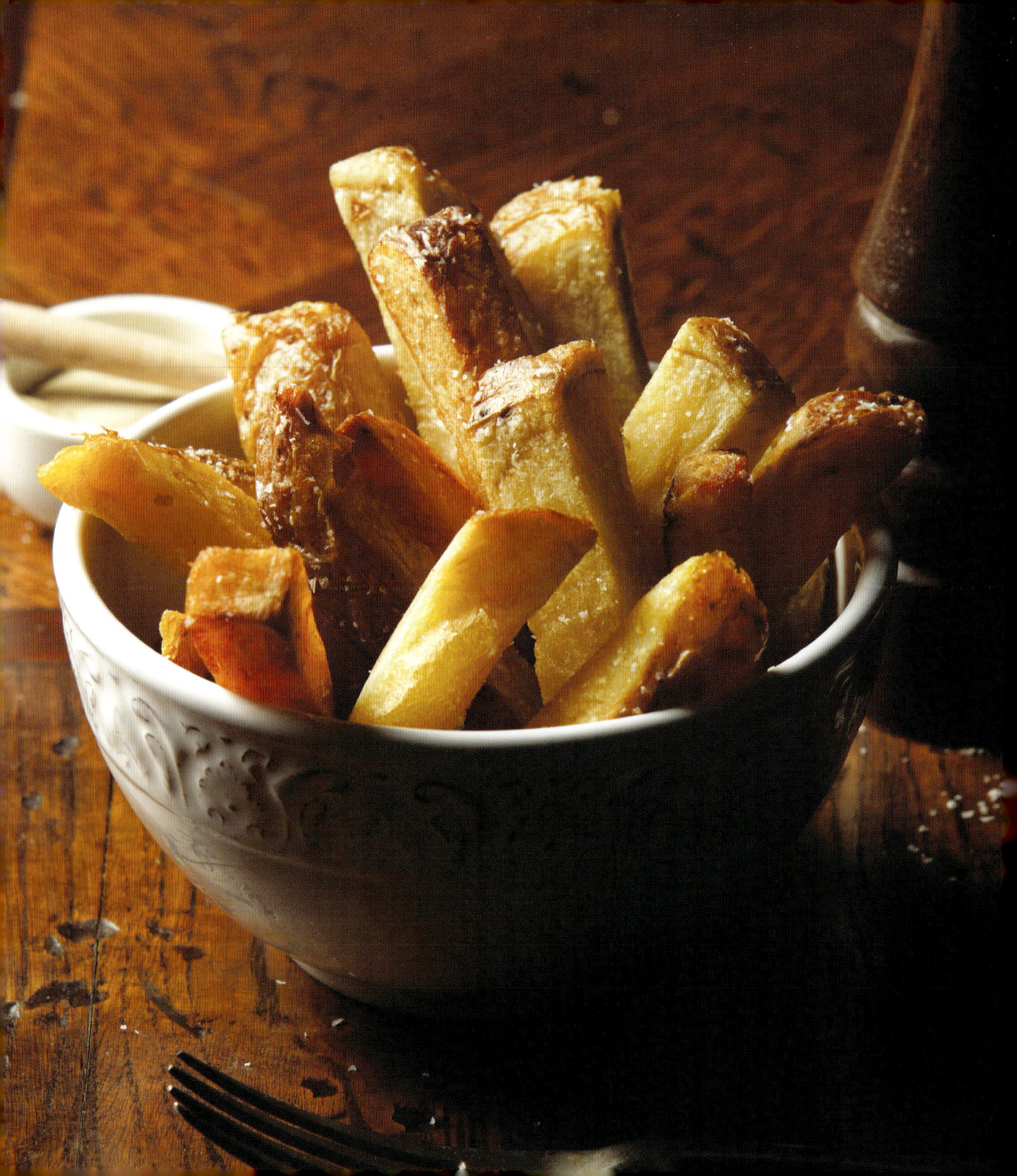

Baked French fries

3 large baking potatoes, skin on, sliced into thick French fries
2 large sweet potatoes, skin on, sliced into thick French fries
1½ tablespoons extra-virgin olive oil
coarse salt and freshly ground black pepper
3 sprigs fresh rosemary, finely chopped

Preheat oven to 220°C/425°F/Gas mark 7.

Toss all the ingredients in a large bowl.

Place on a baking sheet and bake for 15 minutes. Using a spatula, turn the fries over and return quickly to the oven. Cook for another 15 minutes, then turn the fries again. Bake for 5 minutes longer or until golden and crisp.

serves 4

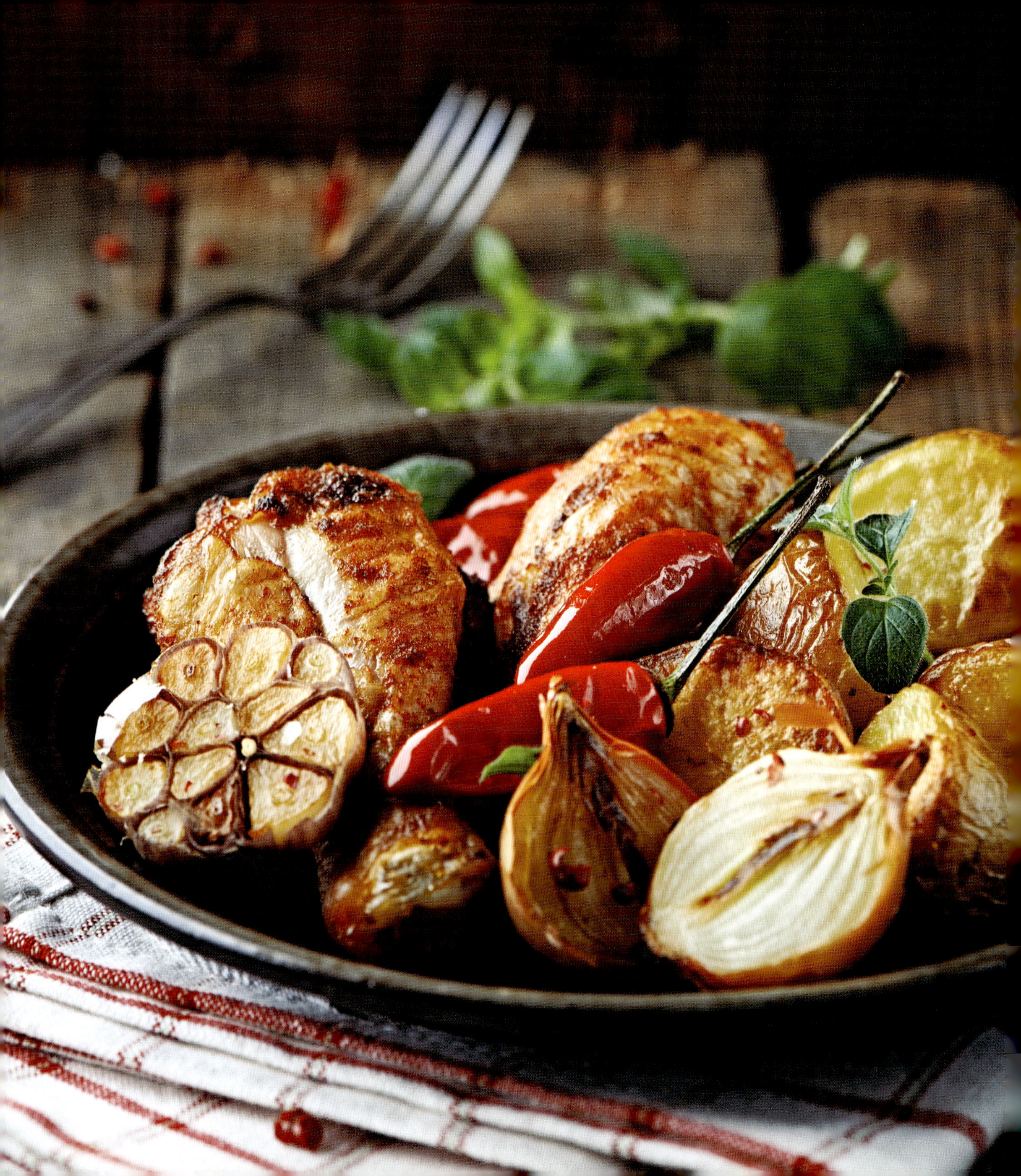

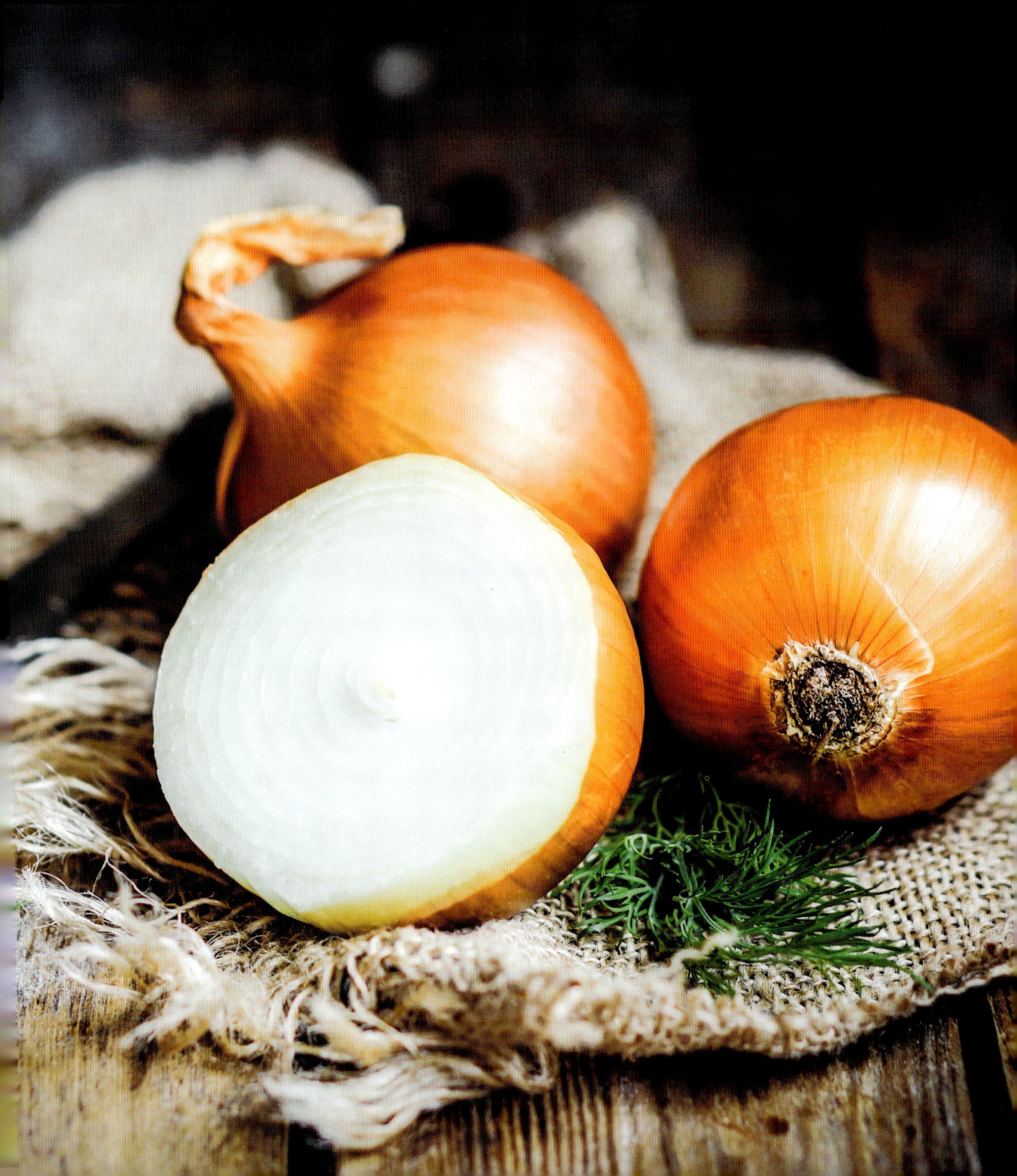

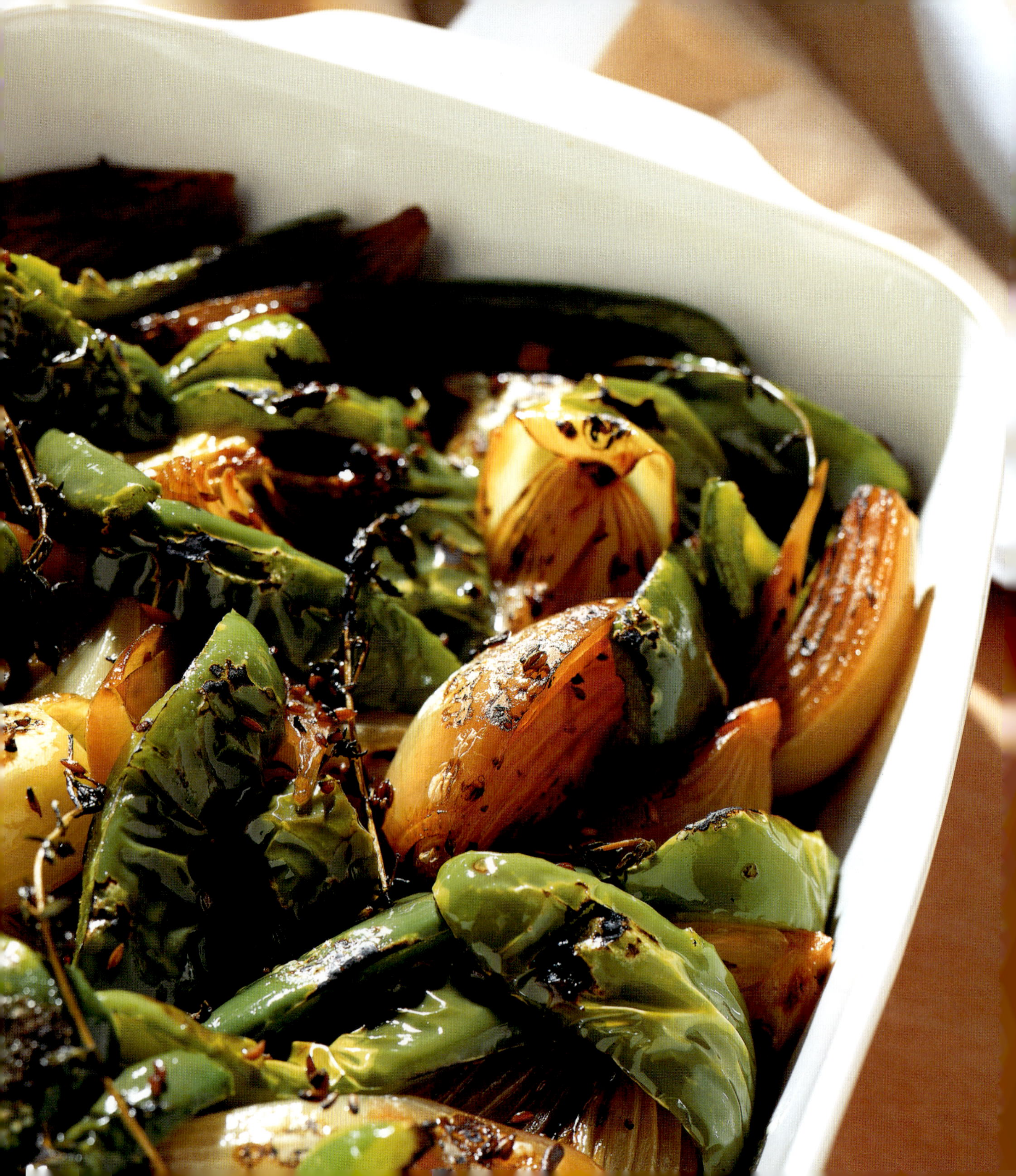

Baked onions and green peppers

4 onions, quartered
3 sprigs of thyme
100 ml/3½ fl oz vegetable stock or white wine
3 tablespoons cider vinegar
2 tablespoons olive oil
1 tablespoon molasses or soft dark brown sugar
2 teaspoons caraway seeds
4 garlic cloves, peeled and left whole
salt and freshly ground black pepper
3 green capsicums (bell peppers), deseeded and cut into wide strips

Preheat the oven to 200°C/400°F/Gas mark 6.

Place the onions, thyme, stock or wine, vinegar, oil, molasses or sugar, caraway seeds and garlic in an ovenproof dish. Season, cover with foil and bake for 30 minutes or until the onions have softened slightly.

Remove the foil, baste the onions with the cooking liquid, then re-cover and return to the oven for 30 minutes, or until the onions are just tender. Add a little water if the liquid has evaporated.

Increase the oven temperature to 240°C/475°F/Gas mark 9. Remove the foil from the dish and stir in the capsicum. Return the dish to the oven, uncovered, and cook the vegetables for 8–10 minutes, turning halfway through cooking, until most of the liquid has evaporated and the vegetables have started to brown.

serves 6

Sides

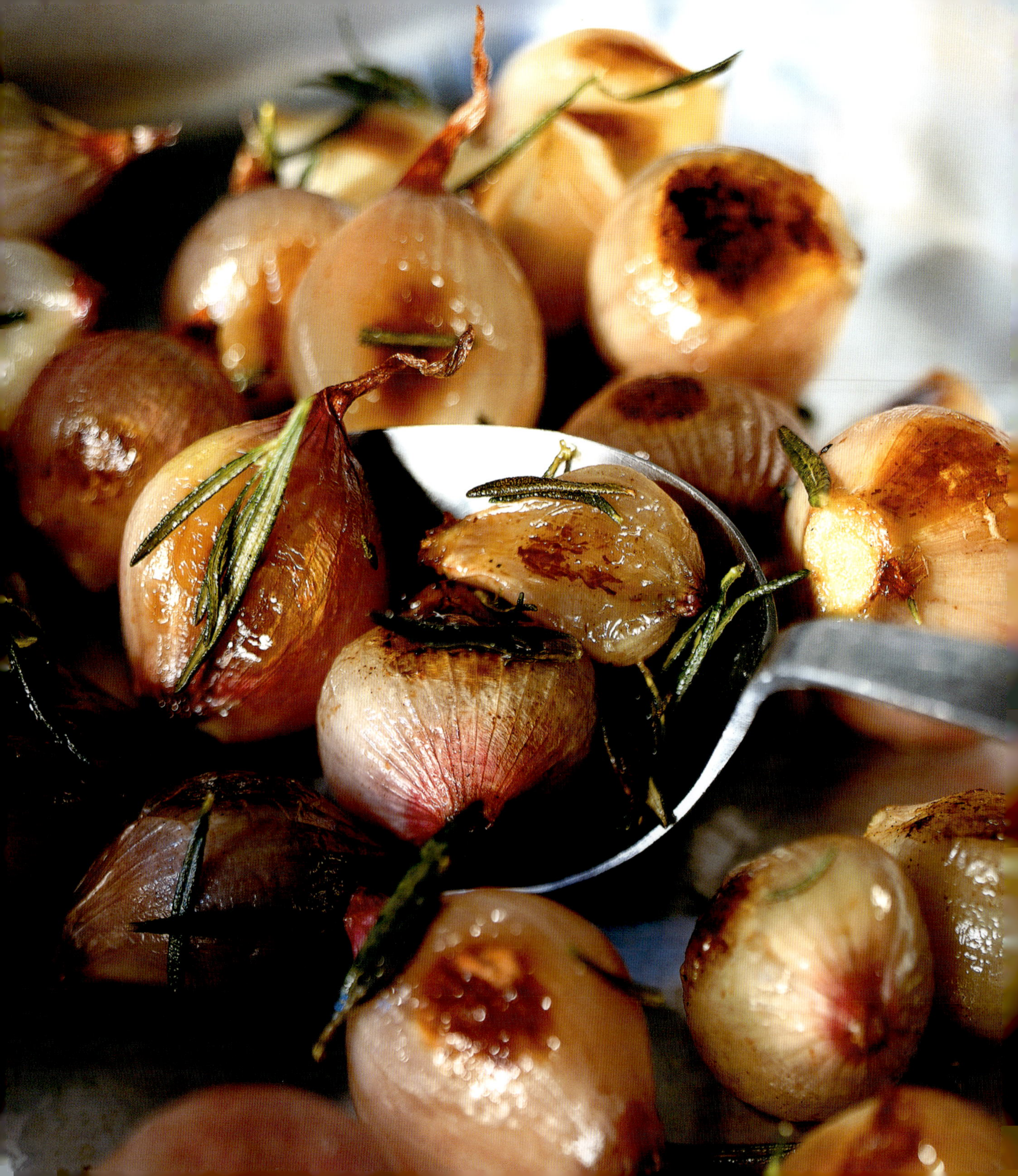

Roasted shallots with rosemary

600 g/1 lb 6 oz shallots or pickling onions
2 tablespoons olive oil
1–2 tablespoons fresh rosemary, chopped
black pepper

serves 4

Preheat the oven to 200°C/400°F/Gas mark 6.

Place the shallots in a roasting tin (pan), drizzle over the oil, sprinkle with the rosemary and black pepper, then toss to mix well.

Bake, stirring once or twice, for 30–40 minutes, until the shallots are tender and golden brown. Serve hot

Sides

Roasted beetroot salad with spinach

24 very small beetroots (beets)
1 tablespoon olive oil
1 tablespoon butter
handful of baby spinach leaves
2 tablespoons balsamic vinegar
100 g/3½ oz hazelnuts, roasted and chopped
2 tablespoons sour cream or natural (plain) yogurt (optional)
freshly ground black pepper, to taste

serves 4

Preheat the oven to 200°C/400°F/Gas mark 6.

Wash the beetroots and scrub them until clean.

Toss the beetroots and olive oil together in a bowl then place them in a baking dish. Cover with foil or a lid and roast for 30–45 minutes, or until tender.

Leave the beetroots to cool, then peel and discard the skin. Cut each in half lengthwise and season with salt and pepper to taste.

Meanwhile, wash the spinach leaves thoroughly then dress with the balsamic vinegar. Transfer the beetroots to a platter or bowl and arrange with the spinach leaves. Scatter over the roasted hazelnuts, adding small dollops of the sour cream or yogurt if desired. Add black pepper to taste.

Sides

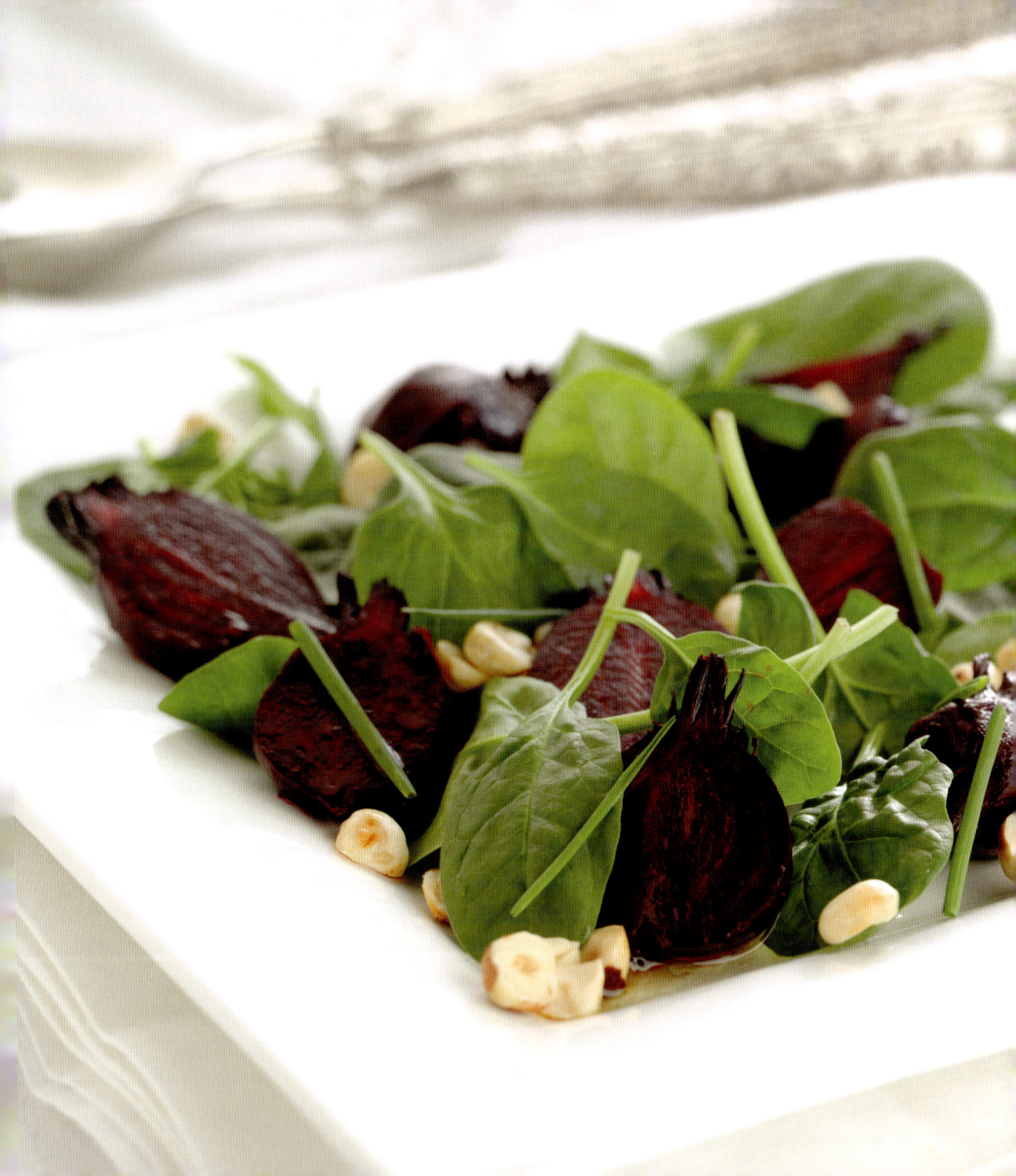

Beetroot, pear and bitter leaf salad

50 g/1¾ oz walnut pieces
200 g/7 oz mixed salad leaves, including radicchio and frisée
225 g/8 oz cooked beetroot in natural juices, sliced
2 pears, quartered, cored and sliced
40 g/1¼ oz Parmesan
fresh chives, to garnish

FOR THE DRESSING
2 tablespoons chopped fresh herbs such as basil, chives, mint and parsley
4 tablespoons walnut oil
2 tablespoons extra virgin olive oil
1 garlic clove, crushed
2 teaspoons red wine vinegar
1 teaspoon clear honey
salt and freshly ground black pepper

Preheat the grill (broiler) to high.

To make the dressing, process the herbs, walnut oil, olive oil, garlic, vinegar and honey until smooth. Season to taste.

Place the walnuts on a baking sheet and grill (broil) for 2–3 minutes, until golden, turning often.

Arrange the leaves, beetroot and pear slices on serving plates. Scatter over the walnuts, then shave over thin slivers of Parmesan, using a vegetable peeler. Spoon the dressing over the salad and garnish with whole chives.

serves 4

Sides

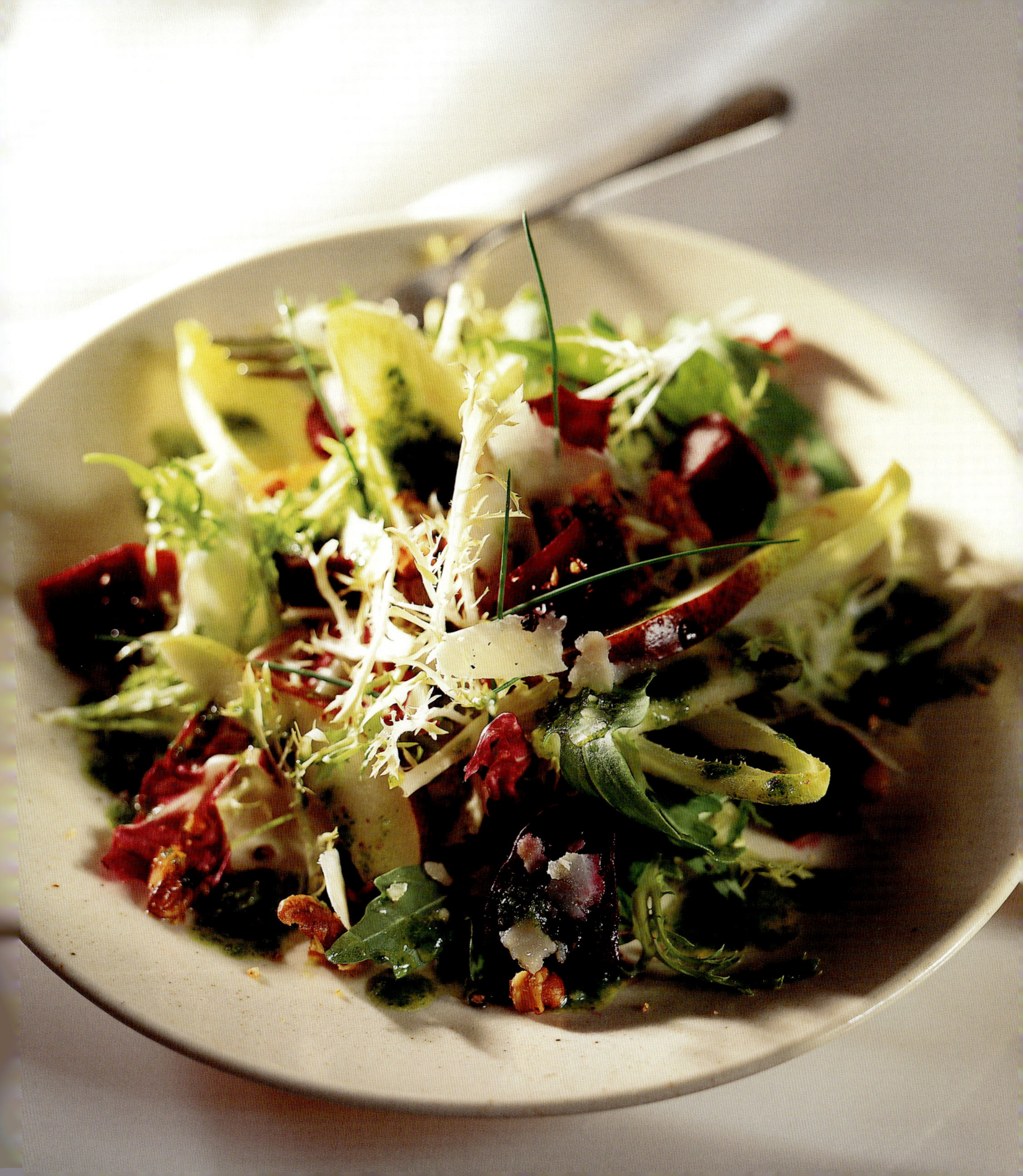

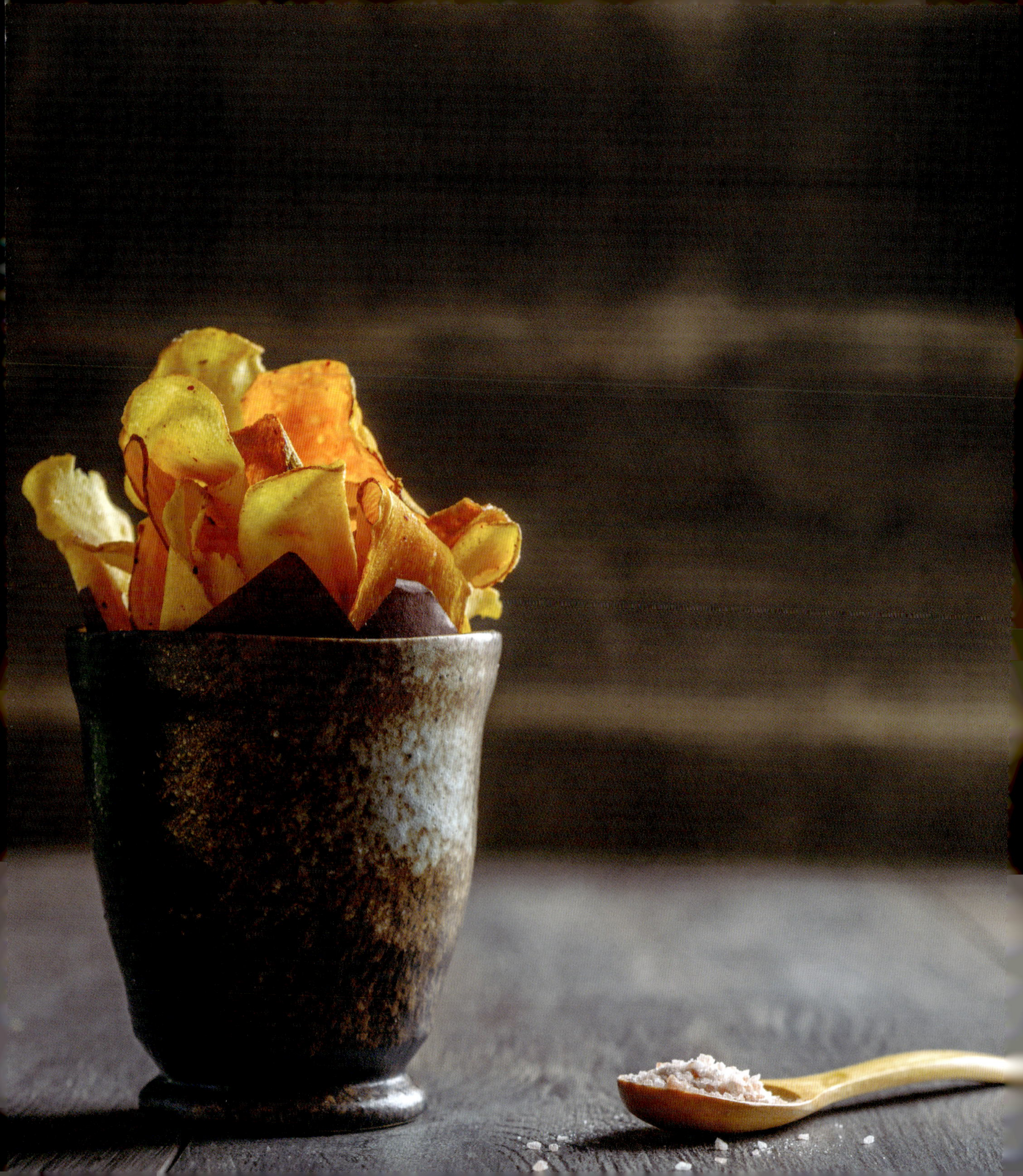

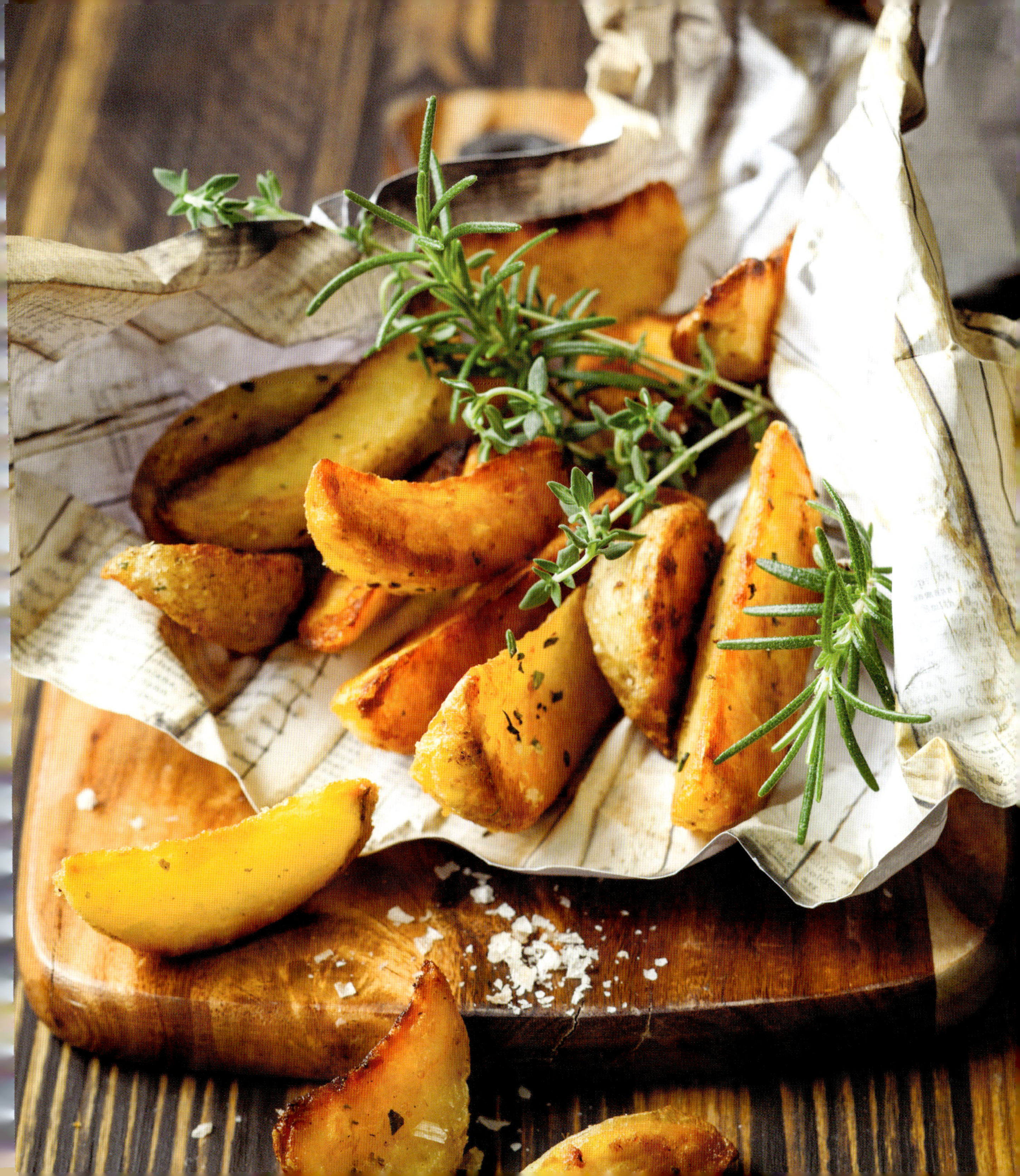

Leeks with beans

250 g/9 oz dried black-eyed (navy) beans, soaked overnight
1 tablespoon vegetable oil
1 large onion, chopped
2 garlic cloves, crushed
450 g/1 lb leeks, sliced and washed
¼ cup/2 tablespoons parsley, chopped, plus extra to garnish
6 tomatoes, peeled, deseeded and chopped
1 tablespoon raw (molasses) sugar
1 teaspoon mustard powder
2 bay leaves
½ teaspoon dried marjoram
1 tablespoon tomato paste
60 ml/2 fl oz/¼ cup vegetable stock
salt and freshly ground black pepper

Drain the beans well. Heat the oil in a frying pan and sauté the onion and garlic, then add the leeks and sauté until softened. Spoon the leek mixture, beans and all the remaining ingredients into slow cooker.

Cover and cook on low for approximately 8–9 hours or on high for 4–5 hours. Garnish with extra parsley.

serves 6

Sides

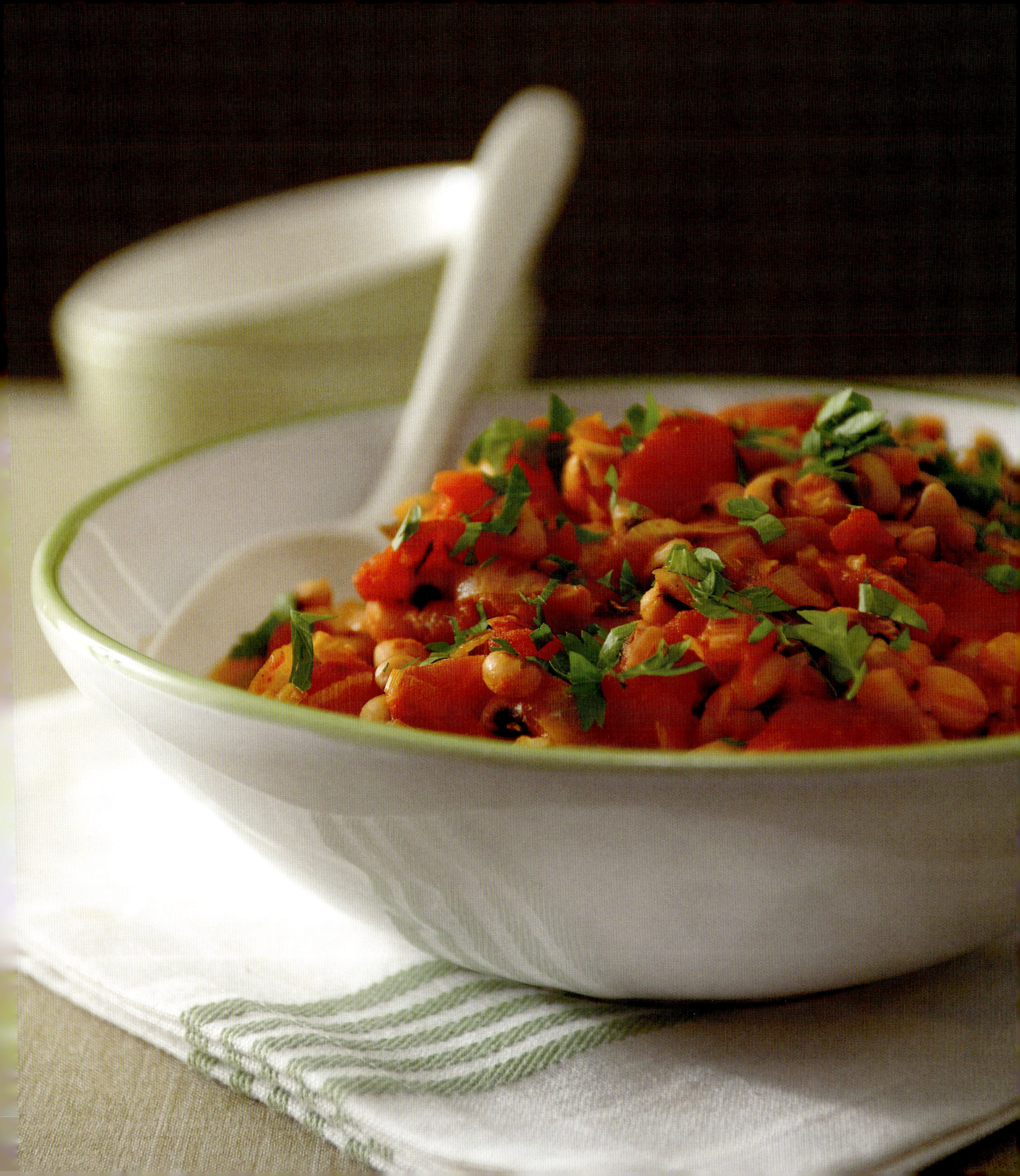

Parsnip mash

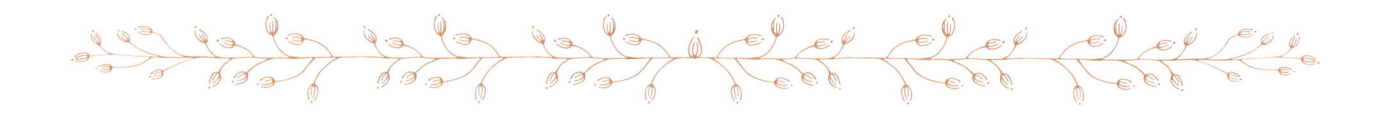

500 g/1 lb 2 oz parsnips, cut into chunks
500 g/1 lb 2 oz floury potatoes, cut into chunks
2 garlic cloves
60 g/2 oz butter
5 tablespoons single (light) cream
salt and freshly ground black pepper
freshly grated nutmeg

Cook the parsnips, potatoes and garlic in a large pan of boiling salted water for 15–20 minutes, until tender. Drain well, then mash with the butter and cream until smooth. Season with salt, pepper and nutmeg.

serves 4

Sides

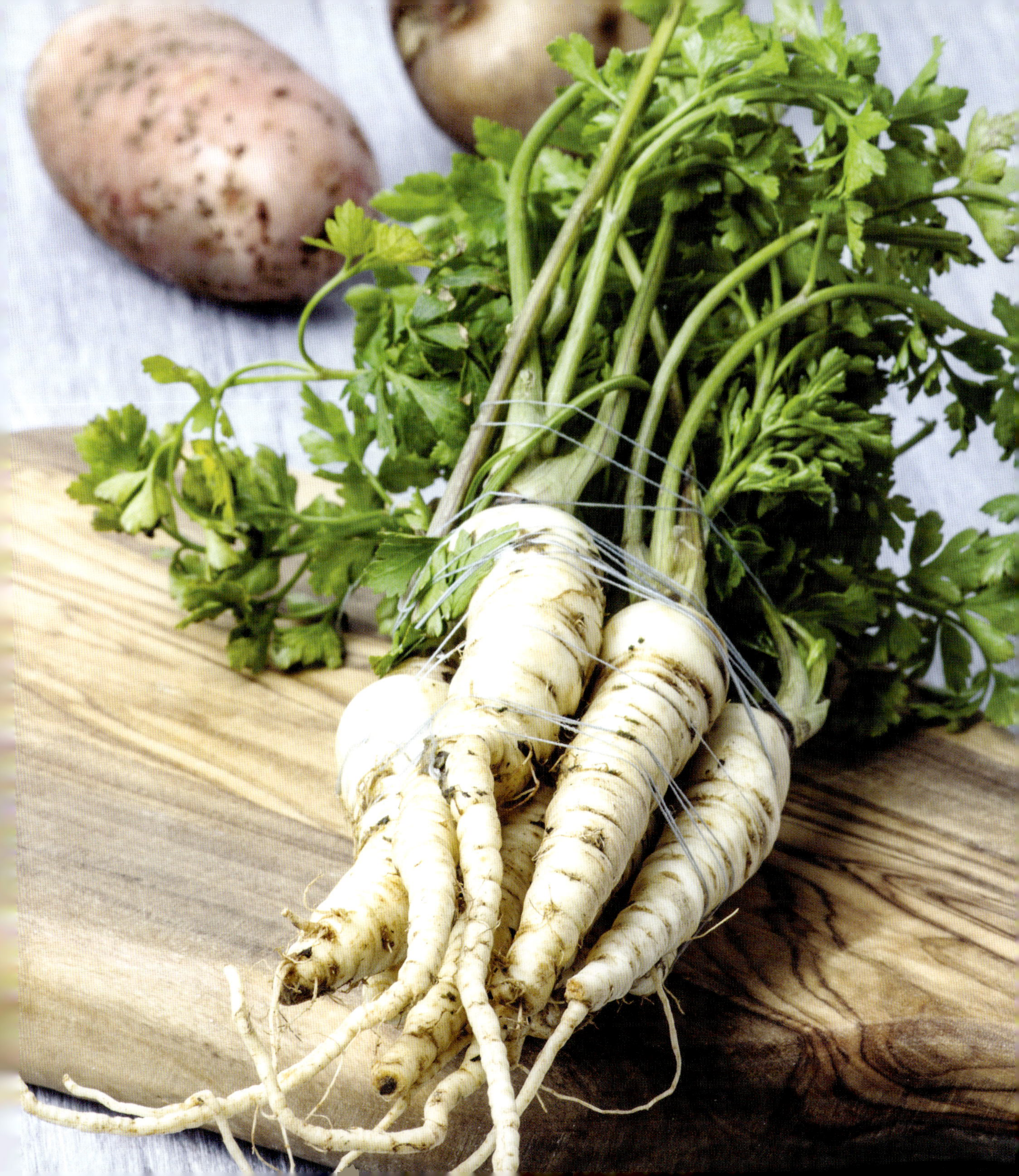

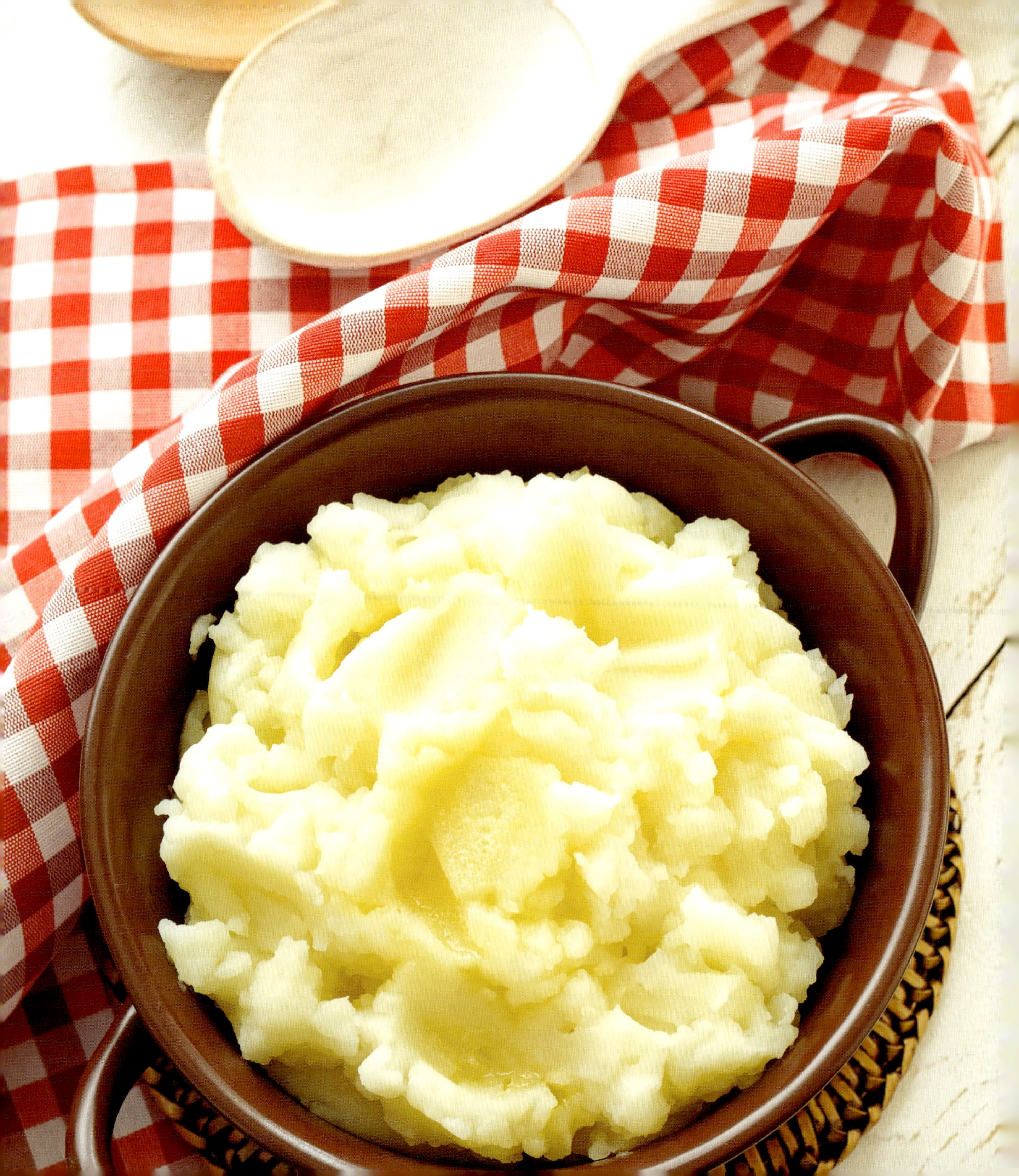

Mashed potatoes

4 medium potatoes, peeled
125 ml/4 fl oz milk
30 g/1 oz
60 g/2 oz cheese, grated (shredded)
salt and freshly ground black pepper, to taste

serves 4

Place the potatoes into a large pan with cold, lightly salted water to cover. Bring to the boil and cook gently, covered, for 20–30 minutes, until the potatoes are easily pierced with a fork. Drain thoroughly, then shake the pan over heat for 1 or 2 minutes until all the surplus moisture has evaporated and the potatoes are dry.

Mash the potatoes, then beat with a wooden spoon until very smooth.

In a pan, heat the milk and butter. Once the mixture is hot, add to the potatoes and beat until light and fluffy. Add the cheese and stir through until melted. Season with salt and pepper. Serve immediately.

Sides

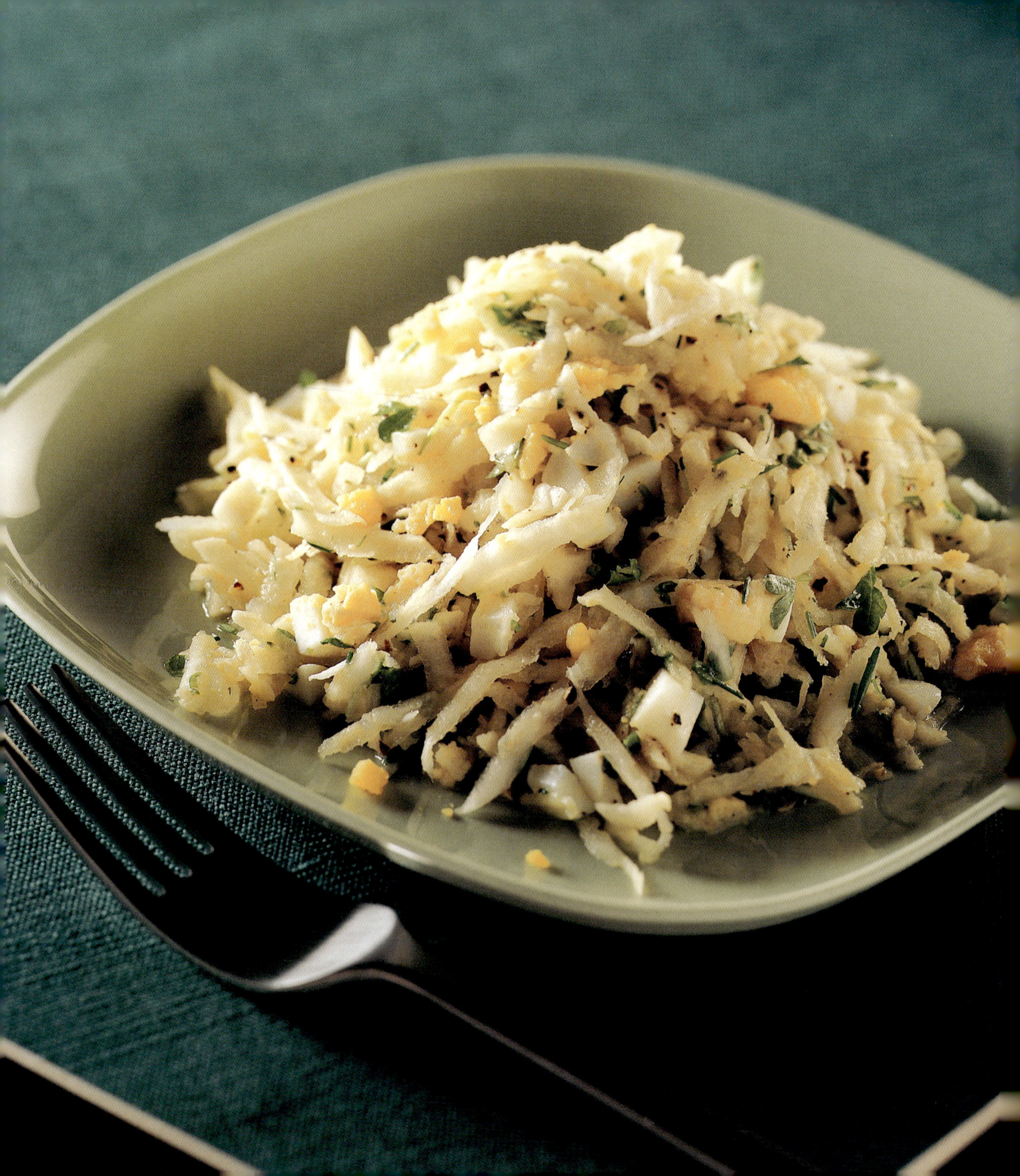

Celeriac and herb remoulade

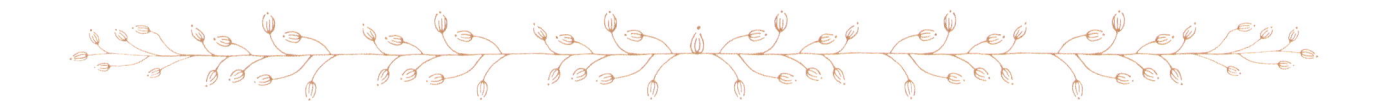

2 eggs
500 g/1 lb 2 oz celeriac, grated
2 tablespoons olive oil
1 tablespoon sesame oil
juice of 1 lemon
3 tablespoons fresh parsley, chopped
3 tablespoons fresh chives, chopped
salt and freshly ground black pepper

serves 4

Bring a saucepan of water to the boil. Add the eggs and boil for 10 minutes. Cool under cold running water, then remove the shells and finely chop the eggs.

Place the celeriac and chopped eggs in a large bowl.

Mix together the olive oil, sesame oil and lemon juice and pour over the celeriac and eggs. Add the parsley, chives and seasoning, then mix thoroughly.

Sides

Index

Baked French fries 149
Baked onions and green peppers 155
Baked onions with mushrooms and pine nuts 71
Beetroot, pear and bitter leaf salad 160
Blue cheese and onion quiche 87
Borscht 23
Brown onion and egg yolk soup 13
Bubble and squeak with onion chutney 63

Caramelised shallot and asparagust toasts 69
Carrot and lentil soup 38
Carrot dip 126
Carrot, lentil and pasta soup 41
Carrots and snowpeas with sesame seeds 144
Celeriac and herb remoulade 173
Cheesy baked potato rösti 151
Cheesy potato frittata 89
Chilli bean potatoes 72

Classic potato salad 139
Coconut, sweet potato and spinach soup 53
Creamed borscht 25
Cumin-spiced carrot soup 36
Curried cream of vegetable soup 48
Curried lentil soup 31

Easy French onion soup 15

Fish pie 97
French onions flans 80
French onions stew 110

Gnocchi with mascarpone and blue cheese 165
Gnocchi with spinach, arugula and basil pesto 109
Grilled pork chops with baked sweet potato 104

Individual sweet potato quiche 66

Lamb and sweet potato stew 107

Lamb shank and vegetable soup 50
Leek, potato and bacon soup 16
Leeks with beans 166

Mashed potatoes 171
Moroccan potato and lemon casserole 101

Parsnip mash 168
Potato and parsley croquettes 79
Potato and pea omelette 90
Potato and bean soup 33
Potato and red onion pizza 115
Potato and sweet potato creamy bake 141
Potato and tomato bake 134
Potato, cheese and onion pie 100
Potato croquettes 77
Potato gratin 150
Potato, onion and bacon cake 112
Potato rösti with smoked trout 64

Index

Provençal-style soup with onion pistou 18

Red onion and chilli tarts 61
Rich vegetable stock 11
Roast potatoes with garlic and rosemary 131
Roasted beetroot salad with dill 158
Roasted leg of lamb with vegetables 118
Roasted new potato pizza 117
Roasted shallots with rosemary 157
Roasted vegetable and broccoli couscous 92
Root vegetable curry 120
Root vegetables and pea soup 28

Shepherd's pie 95
Spiced potato and onion soup 43
Spiced potatoes 147
Spicy carrot salad 128
Stuffed baked potatoes 74
Swede and carrot soup 46

Sweet potato and rosemary soup 55
Sweet potato and onion layered bake 164
Sweet potato, pasta and leek soup 51
Sweet potatoes with sage 133

Vegetable and lentil curry 102

Warm herbed potato salad 136
Watercress and potato soup 26

Index

First published in 2015 by New Holland Publishers Pty Ltd
London • Sydney • Auckland

The Chandlery, Unit 9, 50 Westminster Bridge Road, London SE1 7QY, United Kingdom
1/66 Gibbes Street, Chatswood, NSW 2067, Australia
Office no 5/39 Woodside Ave, Northcote, Auckland 0627

www.newhollandpublishers.com

Copyright © 2015 New Holland Publishers Pty Ltd
Copyright © 2015 in text: New Holland Publishers Pty Ltd
Copyright © 2015 in images: New Holland Publishers Pty Ltd

All rights reserved. No part of this publication may be reproduced, stored in a retrieval system or transmitted, in any form or by any means, electronic, mechanical, photocopying, recording or otherwise, without the prior written permission of the publishers and copyright holders.

A record of this book is held at the British Library and the National Library of Australia.

ISBN: 978 1 742576800

Managing Director: Fiona Schultz
Editor: Simona Hill
Designer: Lorena Susak
Production Director: Olga Dementiev
Printer: Toppan Leefung Printing Ltd
10 9 8 7 6 5 4 3 2 1

Keep up with New Holland Publishers on Facebook
www.facebook.com/NewHollandPublishers